THE

DIY

GUIDE TO

Powerful
Publicity

THE

DIY

GUIDE TO

Powerful
Publicity

Moi Ali

DSC

Published by
Directory of Social Change
24 Stephenson Way
London NW1 2DP
Tel. 08450 77 77 07; Fax 020 7391 4804
E-mail publications@dsc.org.uk
www.dsc.org.uk
from whom further copies and a full books catalogue are available.

Directory of Social Change is a Registered Charity no. 800517

First published 2006

ISBN-10 1 903991 73 0
ISBN-13 978 1 903991 73 2

British Library Cataloguing in Publication Data

A catalogue record for this book is available from the British Library

Cover design by Kate Bass
Typeset by Keystroke, 28 High St, Tettenhall, Wolverhampton
Printed and bound by Page Bros, Norwich

All Directory of Social Change departments in London:
08450 77 77 07

Directory of Social Change Northern Office:
Research 0151 708 0136

Contents

About the Author vii

Foreword viii

Introduction ix

PART 1

Chapter 1 What are words worth? 3

Why is good copy a must? 3
Overcome the fear 5

Chapter 2 Planning and research 9

Audience: remember your reader 9
Establishing your purpose 12
Defining action 13
Tone 13
The message 14
Features and benefits 14
USP: be unique 15
Psychology: fear and rewards 15
Writing the brief 16

Chapter 3 Getting started: putting pen to paper, mouse to mat 20

Six simple stages 20
Starting over 27
Writer's block remedies 27

Chapter 4 Writing that packs a punch 31

First person 31
Don't tell – show 32
Contractions 33
Situational copy 33
Words with personality 35
Plain English 35
Keep active 36
Bite-sized chunks 37

Chapter 5 The dreaded grammar and English 43

Common grammatical mistakes 44
How good is your grammar? 48
English 49
Commonly misused words 52
Sentences 54
Tenses 55
Inclusive language 56

Chapter 6 Time-tested copywriting devices 58

Alliteration 58
Puns 59
Assonance 60
Rhyme 60
Ellipsis 61
Homonyms, heterophones and homophones 61
Antonyms 62
Unexpected deviance 63
Malapropisms 63
Spoonerisms 64

Chapter 7 Common copywriting mistakes and how to avoid them 65

Over-long text 65
Repetition 67
Clichés 68
Very 69
Ambiguity 69
Hype 70
Pomposity 71
No offence intended 71

Chapter 8 Becoming a copy critic 75

Seven simple steps to copy awareness 75
Have a go yourself 76
The bad 76

The good *78*
Comparing notes *79*

Chapter 9 Finding the creative you *84*

Inspiration and ideas *84*
Word games *85*
Subway prophets *85*
Getting your surroundings right *85*
Creativity-boosting exercises *85*

Chapter 10 Words and design in harmony *94*

Make the most of words *95*
When to give more emphasis to
   design than copy *100*
Working with designers *100*
Types of typo *100*
Checking what comes back *101*
Have a go yourself *102*

PART 2

Chapter 11 Direct mail *107*

The envelope *108*
The enclosures *108*
Lead-generating letters *112*
Information letters *113*
Navigational letters *113*
Easy action *114*
Targeting *114*
Reply cards *114*

Chapter 12 Advertising *116*

AIDA *116*
How we 'read' adverts *118*
The body text *122*
Dominance of design *123*
Classifieds *124*
Keep it legal *125*
Bus adverts *126*
Radio ads *126*

Chapter 13 Writing for the web *128*

Providing for scanners *128*
Effective e-mails *130*

Chapter 14 News releases *132*

What is a release? *132*
Ingredients of a successful release *134*
The five Ws *135*
News release musts *138*
Looking the part *138*

Chapter 15 Articles and features *140*

Ideas for openers *141*
Types of reader *142*
The end *142*

Chapter 16 Newsletters *144*

Staff newsletters *144*
Customer/supporter newsletters *146*
Cover page *148*

Chapter 17 Annual reports *149*

Legal requirements *150*

Chapter 18 Catalogues *152*

Providing reassurance *153*

Chapter 19 Leaflets *154*

General purpose leaflets *154*
Information leaflets *155*
Sales leaflets *155*
Booking leaflets *155*
The front cover *155*

Chapter 20 Everything else! *158*

Coupons and response mechanisms *158*
Instructions *158*
Packaging *160*
Captions *162*
Notices *162*
Posters *163*
Speech writing *163*
Writing for foreigners *164*

Appendix: Improvement in writing
   ability 166

Index 169

About the Author

Moi Ali runs her own communications consultancy, The Pink Anglia Public Relations Company, which specialises in public relations, communications and marketing services for voluntary organisations and small businesses. She also runs training courses on writing skills. Moi has more than 20 years' experience in public relations and promotional marketing, working in-house for companies and voluntary organisations, as well as in PR/marketing consultancies.

Moi has tackled a wide variety of copywriting assignments, ranging from leaflets and annual reports to websites and books. Although she has no formal training as a copywriter, over the years she has gained considerable experience in writing powerful publicity material. Her aim here is to condense those years of experience into the following pages, passing on to readers the knowledge she has built up over more than two decades.

Foreword

Copywriting is a deceptive skill. After all, how difficult can it be to write a few words of publicity material? We all write, so what is the problem?

I receive a large daily mailbag of letters, e-mails and press releases, most of which attempt to persuade me that an organisation has a 'really good story'. Much of this material sadly falls at the first hurdle for one simple reason: the copy fails to grab my attention.

Whether you are seeking donations for a charity, volunteers for a project or running a marketing campaign, well-constructed prose enhances the chances of reaching your target audience. As Moi Ali writes in this book, 'Good copy is read; bad copy is binned'.

The good news is that you can learn the necessary skills to turn out readable copy. A DIY guide such as this one provides you with the tools to produce copy that demands to be read.

Just as important is choosing the most appropriate form in which to deliver your publicity, and there is sound advice contained in Part 2 to help you decide the most appropriate way to convey your message.

Organisations work to tight budgets and producing your own publicity material is often the only option. That does not mean it cannot be effective. The basic skills for writing already exist in your head. With careful attention to the craft of copywriting, you can enhance your writing abilities and learn how to communicate your message successfully.

For charities, and voluntary and community organisations, a successful publicity campaign is a crucial element in achieving a goal. If your copy is concise, considered and correct, you will maximise the opportunities to reach your objective.

Jeremy Vine
Editor, *Public Agenda*,
The Times

Introduction

It must be hell running a Weight Watchers class, with group upon group of chubbies scrutinising every inch of your body for excess fat. They expect you to practise what you preach: a flabby midriff is effectively an admission that you're no good at what you do. Although it's OK for writers to have a spare tyre (thankfully!), I still have considerable sympathy for diet and fitness gurus and the pressure on them to embody (literally) what they promote. Why? Because it's like that for me too. Here I am setting myself up as an expert, telling *you* how to write. You'll expect me to demonstrate through my own writing all the things I will be urging you to do. I will be judged harshly. You will be on the lookout for my errors and inconsistencies. You will demand writing excellence – and so you should! You will be more critical of my style than if I were writing a book on gardening or chess. Talk about being under the spotlight! But it's OK. You see, one of the best ways of becoming a better writer is to analyse and criticise the work of others. Learn from what they get wrong. Copy what they do well.

Few people have formal copywriting training, yet many are required to write powerful publicity material of one sort or another – letters to customers or donors, information for the website, a contribution to the annual report or supporters' newsletter. Does this sound like you? It used to be me too. I learned copywriting the hard way: by trial and error over a number of years. I'd like you to learn it the easy (or perhaps I should say 'easier') way. This book will give you the training you (and I) never had. It condenses years of experience into a volume that can be read from start to finish in the time it takes to travel from Portsmouth to Edinburgh by train. So if you want to short circuit the learning curve, this book is for you!

Split into two parts, the first covers theory in an accessible and jargon-free way. As well as outlining various dos and don'ts, the section looks at planning, audiences and style, and reveals the copy-writer's tricks and techniques. Part 2 examines chapter by chapter the main pieces of publicity material you are likely to have to write – news releases, press ads, fundraising and sales letters and so on – and explains how to produce the very best of each.

This book will not transform you into the William Shakespeare of marketing copy, but it *will* dramatically improve your copywriting skills and it *will* boost your confidence. It will guide, advise and encourage you. It will help you develop and fine tune your writing ability quickly and efficiently, fast-tracking you towards your ultimate goal of really powerful publicity. That's what's on offer from this book, but the magic ingredient is YOU. The book will provide the tips, but there's more to compelling writing than the mechanical following of a formula. It is up to you to throw in the time, enthusiasm and commitment to improve your copywriting. You put in the effort and together we can be a powerful team. So read on and watch yourself improve.

PART ONE

What are words worth?

In this chapter, find out why good copy is vital and what you risk if you get it wrong. Discover how to overcome the fear and anxiety many people experience when they have to write publicity material. Complete a fun assessment of your own writing ability.

Many organisations put enormous effort into selecting the best mailing list, choosing the right media for their advertising, or the more arresting photographs for a brochure, only to let poor copy spoil their hard work. Well-targeted mailings or attractively designed publicity materials will fail in their purpose if they are badly written. Your entire marketing, awareness-raising or fundraising campaign will be undermined. Much of the time, effort and money invested may be wasted.

Why is good copy a must?

- Good copy is read: bad copy is binned.
- Good copy can persuade, influence, inform and educate.
- It can lead to enhanced donations and sales.
- Good copy can boost the image and reputation of an organisation.
- Good, clear copy is essential for effective communication, averting the kind of misunderstanding that can lead to ill will between a supporter or customer and an organisation/charity.
- Powerful publicity can help distinguish your organisation from competing causes.
- Often the written material an organisation produces is the first or only contact someone will have with it. It will be used as the basis for deciding whether they want further contact: the whole enterprise will be judged on the basis of the copy. Get it wrong and you will lose potential supporters/customers.

- People are more marketing-savvy today than in our parents' generation. While they don't expect to see charities wasting money on expensive gimmicks, neither do they expect the design and content of marketing and fundraising material to be amateurish. The same goes for small businesses – look amateurish and people may conclude that your business is unprofessional.

It's obvious that good copy is essential. So how come so much poor copy makes it into print? There are two possible reasons. First, many people simply underestimate the vital contribution that good copy can make to a marketing or fundraising programme. They are so preoccupied with creative design, clever mailshots or eye-catching exhibitions that they overlook the foundation stone upon which all of these are built: good copy. Sometimes the words are almost an after-thought, with an over-emphasis on the more glamorous and tangible aspects of a campaign, at the expense of good copy.

Another explanation is that many people have difficulty in distinguishing bad copy from good. They do not find it easy to understand what makes some writing powerful and other prose painful. Some are particularly blind when it comes to their own writing. Yes, it may seem rather a damning judgement, but I have come across many people unable to see the shortcomings of their own work.

Then there are the people like you! You are persuaded of the value of good copy and aware that your own skills could be more polished. You want to find out how you can start writing really powerful publicity.

After years at school studying grammar, spelling, and punctuation, in theory all of us should be able to write well. In practice it was probably those English lessons that turned many of us off writing. All that syntax, those complicated rules about sentence construction, verbs, adverbs, and prepositions . . .! If your ability to write, and to enjoy writing, is blighted by distant memories of school compositions and scary grammar lessons, take heart. Some of the seemingly inflexible rules drummed into you in English lessons can be cast aside and together we can make a clean start.

My aim is to liberate you from the stifling influence of your English teacher (apologies to the good English teachers out there!). I want to free the creativity within you and unlock your writing power. So shake off any belief that you can't write. You can! All you need is plenty of practice, a little confidence building, and a liberal helping of trade secrets. Before long you will be writing powerful fundraising or sales letters, persuasive adverts, and really readable promotional material. Just follow the easy steps described, pick up some tips along the way, and overnight (well almost!) you will be writing publicity that packs a punch.

Overcome the fear

Some people do not believe that they can write well. A few are too afraid even to try. Fear prevents most of us from taking up dangerous sports. Jumping off the Forth Roadbridge supported by an elastic band might result in death: having a go at drafting a press advert will not. So set aside any fears and anxieties. There's no harm in having a go.

Begin by recognising any nervousness or apprehension you have when it comes to writing. Be comforted by the fact that you are quite normal. A straw poll of a dozen acquaintances revealed that 11 of them found writing promotional material both difficult and time-consuming. Accept that you are not alone and cast off your anxiety: it's nothing more than a barrier preventing you from fulfilling your potential. Concentrate on boosting your writing skills and you will find that your confidence grows.

Too many people think that good writers are born. It's an easy excuse for them to give up without trying. True, a few people are blessed with a natural ability to write: the rest of us have to learn. But learn we can. So don't write yourself off as a no-hoper. Sure, there's an art to writing great fiction and few of us could hope to be on a par with George Elliot or Leon Tolstoy, but writing for publicity material is a different kettle of fish. In large part it is a skill that can be learned by any reasonably intelligent adult. Yes, even you! Once you have acquired the skill, it's all down to creativity. That's the factor that distinguishes the technically competent from the great. This book will give you the technical competence and it will nurture any innate creativity you have. In short, it will turn you into a better copywriter.

But let's start with where you are now. Begin by assessing your current writing ability as a benchmark. You can reassess it at the end of the book to see if you have gained in skill and confidence. If this book is worth the paper it's written on, you will see an overall improvement.

Work through the following questions. Select only *one* answer for each question – the one that most closely encapsulates how you feel – then tot up your score at the end.

Current writing ability: self-assessment test

1. I would rate my writing ability as:

a) Poor.
b) Slightly below average.
c) Average.
d) Slightly above average.
e) Good.
f) Excellent.

2. I find getting started:

a) Impossible.
b) Very difficult.
c) Fairly hard.
d) Not hard, but not easy.
e) Fairly easy.
f) Very easy.

3. When I am asked to write some marketing or fundraising material
   I feel:

a) A sense of dread and panic.
b) Genuinely worried that I will make a mess of it.
c) That it will be a struggle and will take time, but I will be able to
   come up with something, albeit second-rate.
d) That I will do an OK job, but not a great one.
e) That I will be able to produce a good piece of work in a reasonable
   timeframe.
f) That it will be a doddle and the output will be great.

4. I think that the publicity material I write is:

a) Dreadful.
b) Poor.
c) Average.
d) Good but could be improved.
e) Above average.
f) Excellent.

5. When it comes to words and language:

a) I have no interest whatsoever in words and how they work.
b) I'm not that interested in words, but very occasionally I will look
   at a piece of publicity and wonder how the creators came up with
   the concept.
c) I have an average interest in words – no more and no less than an
   average person.

d) From time to time I look at/analyse/think about other people's creative work.

e) I enjoy reading and thinking about professional copy and find myself doing it frequently.

f) I am very interested in words and I find language fascinating.

6. When it comes to writing marketing and fundraising material (donor letters, press ads, brochures, annual reports):

a) I find it difficult to write anything and always feel dissatisfied with the end result.

b) I have trouble getting started and rarely like the finished material.

c) I can write some types of marketing material to a reasonable standard, but find others considerably more difficult.

d) I can write most types of material competently, but feel there's room for improvement.

e) I am confident that I can tackle most assignments without too much difficulty and can produce good work.

f) I can turn my hand to anything with ease, always producing very good work.

7. How long does it take you to write, say, a one page fundraising letter, or some other short piece of marketing material, to a good standard?

a) It takes me far too long. I have trouble getting started; I pore over it and never feel that it is any good.

b) It takes me a lot longer than it should, but I get there in the end.

c) I take a bit longer than I would like and feel there is room for improvement.

d) My speed is OK.

e) I can produce good work within an acceptable timescale.

f) I can turn out quality work quickly and easily.

Scores

Now add up your score. Award yourself:

One point for every a) you ticked
Two for every b)
Three for a c)
Four for a d)
Five for an e)
Six for an f)

Assessment

Read the paragraph that refers to your score.

7–12

Either you really are as bad at writing as you think you are, or you have extremely low self-esteem! This is a poor score, but the good news is that it can only go up. There is much you can learn to enhance your skills and build your confidence. You should see a dramatic increase in your score by the end of the book.

13–19

You fall into the slightly 'below average' category. Your writing is not that good, but it's not that bad either! You don't find it easy to write and you are not too confident about the end result. Never fear. After reading this book, you will have bags more confidence and you will find getting started so much easier. You will also be happier with the result.

20–34

This is an 'average' to 'above average' score. Your writing is fine, but there is room for improvement. You can get started with relative ease and you turn out acceptable work. However, you could be faster and a bit slicker. You will be by the end of the book.

35 to 42

Wow! You are so talented! You should be writing this book, not reading it!

This test is semi-serious. It gives you a rough idea of where you stand in the scheme of things. Once you have worked your way through the book, repeat the test (it is reprinted at the end). See how your confidence and ability have grown.

Planning and research

Before you put pen to paper, do some research. This chapter will help you identify who you are writing for, what you want to say to them, and what action you hope they will take as a result.

Professional copywriters rarely write fluent, flowing and perfectly polished prose straight off. If only! I didn't knock out this book in a couple of weeks. Many hard months were spent in its planning and research, with draft upon redraft produced. On a smaller scale, that's what is required if *you* want to write sizzling copy for your fundraising or promotional materials. Do some spadework before you start to write. Give consideration to:

- **Audience** – Who you are writing for.
- **Purpose** – What you hope to achieve through your written material.
- **Message** – The key points you must convey.

Begin to write only after you have completed this initial thinking/ researching/planning stage. Inexperienced copywriters feel failures because they cannot sit down with a blank sheet of paper (or clear computer screen) and instantly churn out startlingly original and creative work. Once they realise that the planning stage is an essential first step, they feel reassured.

Audience: remember your reader

No one can write appropriately without regard to their audience. Consider who you are writing for. Each audience will have distinct needs, interests and preferences. Identify your audience and you are a step closer to tailoring the content of what you write.

Sometimes you will write material for one clearly defined audience. More often you will be called upon to produce material for a diverse audience, posing more challenges for the writer.

A common mistake is to forget the reader. It's easily done. You may be so wrapped up with your company, charity or cause that you completely overlook the poor old reader, struggling to make sense of it all (or giving up altogether and chucking your work in the bin). If you don't make a conscious effort to remember your reader, they won't remember you (or they will, but for all the wrong reasons). Forget your reader and you might as well be talking to yourself. Talking to yourself is not communicating; talking to others is.

When you write to your Great Aunt Mildred, she wants to read what you have to say, eager for news of her favourite niece or nephew. The person reading your leaflet will not have your great aunt's avid interest in you. They may not be interested in you at all, or your organisation. Your job is to get them interested – early on – and to keep them reading. To achieve this you must remember your reader as you write. Aim for riveted readers, but remember that riveted readers require riveting writing.

When sitting down to write a new leaflet, an annual report or any other material, begin by asking yourself who ultimately will read it. Ensure your answer is as specific as possible. 'Supporters' is too vague. Will they be wealthy? Students? Young and single? Grandparents? Mainly male? Organisations with a slick fundraising or marketing operation will already have an accurate picture of the typical supporter/customer in the form of a donor/ customer profile. The donor or customer profile will help you tailor your material so that it has maximum appeal for the target audience. If you do not have this facility, do your own research. Find out as much as you can about your readership.

Attempt to get inside your reader's head. What will make them sit up and take notice? What interests them? What situation are they in? How much time do they have to deal with your mailing or your advert? Are they being bombarded with similar material from other organisations? Are they in a busy office with competing demands on their time? Are they retired, at home, and with loads of free time on their hands? Are they at home and stressed out looking after screaming children? Think about what they will be doing when they read your publicity material. Imagine how they might be feeling. Recall all of this when you come to write. Ignore the needs of your audience, and the pressures on them, and your publicity may also be ignored.

Generally you will find that a particular group will have its own needs, wants, preferences and pressures. Take the example of a manager in a large company, to whom an organisation is writing for support with a charity event:

tip

Think about whether you know anyone who fits your target audience. Write for them. It is always easier to write for a real person than for an abstract classification such as 'AB males under 35'.

Managers: their situation

- Managers are busy people.
- They receive a lot of mail, especially unsolicited material.
- Secretaries usually open their mail.
- Most managers want to clear their in-trays. It is easier to throw away complicated publicity material than read it.
- It is quicker to discard anything not immediately relevant than spend time searching for relevance.
- Managers usually have a great deal of professional reading to do – reports, trade publications and so forth. You will be competing with this.

Managers: their needs

- Managers want the benefits clearly spelt out early on.
- They want relevant information that will help them or their business.
- They want material tailored to their profession/position or company, so they know immediately that your communication is relevant.
- They need information that is short and to the point: they don't have time to wade through heavy or complex copy.
- They want everything set out in an easy-to-digest format, with lots of bulletpoints, boxed text and other devices to draw their eye to key points.
- They don't want padding and waffle.
- They are happy with the use of their own trade jargon, but not other jargon.

By contrast, look at the position of a potential donor (one that fits the charity's donor profile):

Potential donor

- They are already interested in the issue or concern, or have a degree of sympathy with it.
- They will be more inclined than other readers to hear what the charity has to say and to consider its message.
- They may be more willing to accept longer copy, *if* it is readable, relevant and informative.
- They may welcome the mailing, be happy to read the charity's advert or make a point of picking up its leaflets.

The same goes for a prospective customer. Someone considering buying a new conservatory will want to read a company's conservatory furniture mailshot. By considering your audience and their needs, you will have a better idea of what your reader wants and of what you should avoid. Were a charity to write to a busy HR manager using copy suitable for a potential donor, it would fall at the first hurdle.

☒ *Dear Ms Lewis,*

> *Anytown Dog Rescue has been helping abandoned dogs in Anytown for more than half a century. In that time, we have aided around 500 dogs by providing free veterinary care and a rehoming service for these sad, often injured and lonely animals.*
>
> *The launch of our Payroll Giving scheme two years ago has proved successful, with more than a dozen local companies signed up. Now we would like to offer your company the opportunity to . . .*

☑ *Dear Ms Lewis,*

> *MOTIVATE YOUR STAFF AND HELP A LOCAL GOOD CAUSE*
>
> *Other companies who support our Payroll Giving scheme have found that it motivates their staff, enhances their company's image and attracts excellent 'feel good' coverage in the local media. Please let one of our fundraisers spend 20 minutes with you explaining the benefits.*

This no-nonsense, straight to the point approach works. It flags up from the outset its relevance and potential benefits. The more ponderous letter above it would end up in the 'wicker filing cabinet': the bin! The writer has probably lost the reader by the end of the first paragraph, as the busy HR manager struggles to work out what abandoned dogs have got to do with her!

Having considered *who* you are writing for, turn your attention to *why* you are writing.

Establishing your purpose

Never produce publicity material for the sake of it. Organisations waste too much time and money turning out unnecessary materials. Stop to consider why you need a new leaflet or brochure. You cannot start on the copy until you have established the purpose of the material you are writing. The purpose of a leaflet might be:

- to persuade
- to inform
- to win support
- to sell
- to educate
- to build an image.

A leaflet aimed at informing will contain lots of facts and information. One designed to persuade will have arguments that build up a persuasive case. Without a clearly defined purpose you cannot choose the right content, or the appropriate words to convey the message in the most powerful way.

Defining action

Getting people to read what you have written is only part of the battle. They must also take action. This might include:

- contacting you for further information;
- making a donation;
- taking out a membership;
- signing your online petition;
- visiting one of your outlets;
- requesting a catalogue;
- placing an order with your company;
- telling other people about what they have read, and spreading the word;
- writing to their MP in support of your cause;
- organising an event to raise money for your charity;
- volunteering their time.

Define what you want the reader to do as a result of reading your material. Clearly spell out what is required.

Tone

When we speak, the listener can hear our tone. Identical words can come across very differently depending on how we say them. The word 'hurry' can be said in an angry or impatient way, in an imploring way, or in a questioning way. Visual clues such as facial expressions and body language reinforce our message. The written word is one-dimensional in comparison. All our meaning must be conveyed in words, without the added help of intonation or non-verbal clues. Decide on tone before you begin writing. How do you want to come across? Friendly and informal? Authoritative? Caring? What sort of personality does your organisation have? What vocabulary and style will help you convey that personality to your reader?

The message

What do you want to say to your readers? What are the key points you must convey? Are there any subsidiary points? Prioritise by identifying the information you *must* get across, and distinguishing this from messages you would find it desirable to communicate. If the copy is too long, delete the desirable and leave in the essential points. Use your list as a checklist, to make sure that you have not overlooked anything important when writing your copy.

Features and benefits

Dull and lifeless copy promotes features. Readers are not interested in features; they want to know about benefits. What's the difference? Well, if you were to promote *features*, you might write:

> ☒ *This craftsman-made sofa has dovetail joints, reinforced with metal rivets driven deep into the sofa's structure, giving it a rigid construction. Additionally the upholstery is double-Scotchsafe coated.*

This copy focuses on the features of the product, such as the way it is made. Features are often of considerable interest to the company producing or selling an item. It may have put great effort into their development, and feel proud of what has been achieved. The punter does not share this interest and could not care less about features; they want to know about the *benefits* of these features.

> ☑ *This craftsman-made sofa is so strong it will outlive you. Its tough, invisible protective coating guards against all spills and stains, so your sofa stays as fresh as the day you bought it – and you'll never have to splash out on expensive shampooing and dry cleaning.*

Now the benefits are clearly spelt out. The feature – dovetail joints reinforced with metal rivets – is presented as a benefit: the sofa is so strong it will outlive you. The double-Scotchsafe coated feature is explained as a benefit: no stains and no expensive shampooing. Don't be a feature-freak. Promote the benefits. If you find it easier, list the features first and then turn them into benefits:

An office chair	
Features	Benefits
Ergonomic design	Won't give you back ache
Fully adjustable	Will be comfortable whatever your height or build
Aluminium frame	Lightweight and easy to move

USP: be unique

USP stands for 'unique selling point' (or unique selling proposition). Your USP is the thing that makes your product or service unique. A USP is valid *only* if it is meaningful to your customers. Having a performance-enhancing piece of machinery is not a USP in its own right; it is merely a means to it. The specialist machinery might enable you to offer a faster service (with dispatch of orders in 12 hours rather than the 48 hours offered by your rivals). Now you have a USP! Base your USP on being:

- the oldest or newest;
- the largest or smallest/most personal;
- the most respected;
- the best on price;
- the best selling;
- the first;
- the most advanced;
- the only provider of that particular service or product;
- able to offer special extras such as a regular customer newsletter containing special offers, a free extended warranty, invitations to pre-sale previews, corporate hospitality.

Psychology: fear and rewards

Good copy works at a psychological level, persuading and influencing. It indicates the reward of buying the product or supporting the cause, presenting it in a way that is designed to appeal to feelings and emotions as well as logic. A copywriter might suggest that a new mascara offers beauty and sophistication, not just thicker lashes. A car is not just a vehicle that will reliably and economically get you from A to B: it offers freedom. A campaign to save wetlands not only offers a protected environment for endangered birds; it will also provide a better world for our children and grandchildren.

Keep copy positive, not negative. Focus on rewards. Text that dwells heavily on what will happen if the customer does not buy can be counter-productive. Sometimes you can get away with subtly hinting that buyers can avoid something unpleasant thanks to your product, thereby fostering the fear factor at a subconscious level. You might hint that the reader will be unfashionable, mean, uncaring, smelly . . . or whatever, if they do not take up your offer. But take care with such an approach, as it may backfire. A blatant fear-promoting statement would be offensive and thus inadvisable, as this fictitious example for an educational bookseller indicates:

x̄ *Reject this special offer and your children's education will suffer. They will fall behind at school and never catch up. You will ensure your children are destined to a life of failure.*

A more subtle approach is required:

☑ *Every parent wants the best for their children. Give yours a head start with our educational books. They will set your children up for a life of learning.*

The message is the same: failure to take up the offer will result in parents giving their children a poorer start in life. The second version presents it more positively, palatably and persuasively. Here's another example, this time a real life advert for panty liners:

[photo of a woman with the headline:]
How do I stay fresh, clean and comfortable all day, every day?

The inference is that without these panty liners the woman would be smelly, dirty and uncomfortable. This device enables the copywriter to say something that would, if stated in a less oblique way, be rejected by the reader as nonsense or as downright insulting.

At this planning stage, identify whether there is a fear factor. Later you can explore how this can be worked into your copy.

Writing the brief

Work through each of the above stages and you will end up with a clear brief for your writing assignment. It may seem a little odd to write a brief for yourself, but without one you may be unclear and unfocused. It is easier to write to a brief because you will be in no doubt about who you are writing for, what they want to know, what key points you need to convey, and what effect you want to produce. To produce a brief for your next assignment, just complete the following:

Write your own brief

Assignment: ....

Audience(s): ....

Audience needs: ....

Purpose of copy: ....

Desired response/outcome: ....

Tone: ....

Benefits: ....

USP: ....

Psychology: ....

Rewards: ....

Fear: ....

Proposition/offer: ....

Here's a completed brief, to illustrate how you might complete each section.

Zoo leaflet brief

Assignment: Zoo leaflet

Audience(s): Parents with young children, living within 90 minutes' drive of the zoo

Audience needs: Bright and attractive, easy-to-digest information, and all the relevant details: opening hours; admission charges, including family tickets; main attractions; practical information such as nappy change, children's meals, car parking and public transport etc.

Purpose of copy:

a) To persuade the reader that the zoo offers a fun yet instructive and value-for-money day out for the whole family.
b) To inform them of the zoo's many attractions and the learning opportunities presented to children visiting it.

Desired response/outcome: To persuade the reader to organise a family day out at the zoo

Tone: Friendly and fun

Benefits:

- A cheap day out: the entrance fee covers all activities (pony rides, face painting etc.) and there's free parking on-site and a free shuttle bus from the nearby town.
- There is more than enough to fill a whole day.
- There's fun for the whole family: attractions for all ages include play areas for toddlers, ecology centre and global warming exhibition for teenagers, restaurant and wildlife cinema for adults.
- It is a stress-free place for parents: the family-friendly environment features nappy change facilities, children's menus, high chairs etc.
- It's educational – children will learn about their world in a fun, hands-on and dynamic way.

USP:

- It is the only zoo with a permanent ecology centre and wildlife cinema.
- It is the only zoo with baby tigers.
- It is the only zoo within a 100-mile radius.

Psychology:

Rewards

- An opportunity to get children interested in the world's animals and in important issues such as ecology and global warming
- A chance to give children an educational trip that is also highly enjoyable and memorable

Fear

If you do not take your family to this zoo you may be neglecting their education and missing an opportunity to equip them with the skills they will need as the future custodians of our planet.

Proposition/offer:

A value-for-money fun day out for the whole family. A family ticket costing just £15 admits two adults and up to four children, making it one of the best and cheapest days out in the county.

Your brief acts as your personal checklist. When you complete the text for your publicity material, revisit the brief and your other planning notes. Have you written in an appropriate style for the audience? Will readers take the necessary action? Have you conveyed the key messages? If you have missed anything, revise your copy. Test-drive your material on a few people. See if they can work out whom it has been written for, what its purpose is, and what the reader should do after reading it.

Getting started: putting pen to paper, mouse to mat

To achieve the perfect piece of copy, you must know how to approach that blank sheet of paper. This chapter shows you how to plan and shape a piece of writing by gathering, organising and grouping ideas. Find out how to draft copy, what to look out for when revising your drafts, and how to fend off writer's block.

Getting started can sometimes be the hardest part of writing. Once you're in full flow it's easy, but composing those first few sentences can be hell. Make it easier for yourself by following these six simple stages.

Six simple stages

- **Gather** – Jot down your thoughts and ideas.
- **Group** – Arrange them into clear themes.
- **Sequence** – Organise themes into a logical order.
- **Place** – Decide what is going where and how much space it should be allocated.
- **Write** – Produce a first draft.
- **Revise** – Work on subsequent drafts and polish your finished work.

Gathering

Stage one in the writing process is the gathering of ideas. Get a piece of paper and jot down all thoughts, ideas and information in note form. Capture anything at all, in any order. Skip this stage and you may find that you are so busy remembering all the thoughts and ideas bombarding your brain that you are unable to concentrate on writing. There's also the risk that you will overlook something important.

Here's an example of what you might come up with during the gathering process:

Stride: Hi-star's running shoe

product name: Stride

professional: used by Olympic runners

benefits

enhances running performance

comfortable

colours

guards against injury

materials

photos of the shoe

sports star endorsement? Top trainer? Olympic gold medallist?

order form

sizes

quality

construction of shoe

The gathering process will leave you with a jumble of thoughts and ideas set out in no particular order. Next you must group related ideas.

Grouping

Look at your notes and group related items into clear themes. Incorporate any new ideas that spring to mind and add detail where you can. Delete anything that now seems irrelevant. You will end up with something like this:

Benefits

Grip-fast polyresin sole enhances running performance

Double-thickness leather upper and ankle support guard against injury

Contoured interior creates the most comfortable running shoe ever

Standard information

Price

Order form

Address

Product details

Sizes

Colours

Materials: leather uppers, polyresin sole

Illustrations

Fashion close-up shot of the shoe, perhaps in a running block

Photo of the shoe in action: runner on track

Computer-generated illustration of interior contours

You have not yet started to write, but it's taking shape. Clear groups/themes are emerging. Edit further at this stage if necessary.

Sequencing

Sort your themes into a clear and logical order. Do this chronologically, alphabetically or in some other sequence that will make sense to the reader. Each new theme or section should lead on logically from the preceding one.

Placing

This stage is not always necessary, depending on what you are producing. With some publicity material, you may need to be clear in your mind about where things are going to go, and how much space each section will be allocated. Take the example of the running shoe leaflet:

A4 sheet folded to A5

Outer cover: Large photo of Roger Bannister holding the shoe. Short pithy quote. Logo. Quote and photo to have equal prominence in terms of design

Inside page 1: Introduction. Explain why Bannister endorsed shoe. Bullet point benefits

Page 2: Company credentials (half a page)

Practical info. – sizes, colours, order details

Back page: order form

By organising the content logically and allocating each theme a slot, you can almost visualise the layout of the finished work as you begin to write.

Writing

At last you are ready to start writing! Reread your brief (see Chapter 2) and look through any notes you created during the sequencing and placing stages. Now produce a first draft. Don't worry about style at this stage: it's only a draft and will be revised several times. Going back to the running shoe example, your first draft might look something like this:

[outer cover]

'If the Stride had been around in my day, perhaps I'd be famous for the three-minute mile!'

[photo of Roger Bannister holding the shoe]

[caption] Sir Roger Bannister, the first runner to complete the four-minute mile

[Logo]

[page 1]

Why top runners choose the Stride

Roger Bannister is a running legend. Although well into retirement, he still runs every day. And the sports shoe he chooses is Hi-star's Stride. He's in good company. Every gold medallist runner in the last

---

Olympics sported the Stride. Why? Because it's the best running shoe you can buy.

Enhance your running performance

The Stride's unique grip-fast polyresin sole won't let you slip or slide, even in wet weather. Now you can run sure and fast every time on every surface in all conditions.

Guard against injury

A double-thickness leather upper, combined with ankle support, protects you from twists and sprains.

Protection from pain

Feel like you're running on air. The Stride's contoured interior makes it *the* most comfortable running shoe ever. No more blisters or sore spots.

[page 2]

Hi-star: Serving runners for decades

We've been manufacturing running shoes for half a century. More professional runners choose Stride, our best shoe ever, than any other shoe by any other manufacturer. That speaks for itself!

Great looks built to last

■ Available in the season's hottest colours: garden green, lipstick pink (up to size 8 only), yellow fizz, ocean blue and, of course, classic and ever-popular black on white.

[show samples of the colours, each clearly labelled]

■ All sizes stocked, including half sizes, from adult size 4 up to size 12.
■ Supple, double-thickness leather uppers allow your feet to breathe, while offering protection and durability. The polyresin sole is hard wearing and cushions your feet, as does the natural cotton contoured insole. Each pair comes complete with our unique, patented no-fray laces.
■ At only £39.95 we beat the competition on price, performance and style.

Ordering is easy. Just complete the form overleaf and return it to us in the postage-paid envelope. Your shoes will arrive within a fortnight, guaranteed.

[back page]

ORDER FORM

Yes! I want to order the shoes professional runners recommend.
Please send me a pair of Hi-star Strides:

Name: . . . .

Address: . . . .
. . . .
. . . .

Size: (from adult 4 up to 12, including half sizes)
. . . .

Colour: (remember 'lipstick pink' is available only up to size 8)
. . . .

Payment

Pay by cheque, debit or credit card.

I enclose a cheque for £ . . . . made payable to Hi-star.

Please charge my debit/credit card (delete as applicable)

Card number:

Expiry date:

Signature:

Return in the post-paid envelope, or post to Hi-star, Freepost LE15
113. Alternatively, debit and credit card orders can be faxed to us on
01123 245541.

Please tick here if you do **not** want to be sent details of other sports
special offers from top manufacturers ☐

After all that planning, the first draft can be something of a
disappointment. But remember that a first draft is a vital starting
point. It won't be perfect so don't expect it to be! Remind yourself
that typed copy on A4 paper, devoid of design input and illustrations,
will always look a bit flat. Good design brings copy to life, so it's OK
if your efforts look a little lifeless at this stage.

Revising

tip

Reread what you have written through the eyes of the intended audience. Check that the style is right for your reader. Ensure your purpose is clear and that the necessary messages are conveyed.

Don't expect to be able to get away with just one draft. You'll need to revise your work a number of times. Put your copy to one side and return to it later, preferably after a few days. You will then find it easier to spot any stilted text, any inappropriate words or sections, and any repetition or omission. An award-winning copywriter said: 'I write my copy the way my grandmother made minestrone soup. I throw in every interesting ingredient I can find and slowly reduce them down.' Reduction (or editing) is vital!

Mark any text you are unhappy with. In particular, look out for:

- **Repetition** – Over-use of the same words or phrases or the same information.
- **Clichés** – Clichés wash over readers, fail to make an impact and should be avoided (unless you are using them in a witty way – 'Now there's no need to cry over spilt milk' [an advert for a stain-resistant carpet] or 'The best thing since sliced bread' [advert for an upmarket uncut loaf]).
- **Anything irrelevant**.
- **Redundant words** – For example, *advance* planning (planning is always done in advance); *work* colleagues (colleagues are people you work with); 6am *in the morning* (it is impossible for 6am to be in the evening).
- **Ambiguity** – Everything should have just one meaning, unless you are deliberately and wittily using *double entendre*.
- **Lack of clarity** – reword to ensure that your meaning is clear.
- **Consistency** – if you hyphenate the word 'co-ordinate' in the first paragraph, do so throughout. Also ensure consistency of words ending in 'ise'/'ize'.
- **Long screeds of unbroken text** – break daunting passages into readable chunks.
- **Omissions** – is anything vital missing?
- **Jargon** – check that the intended audience will understand any jargon you have used.
- **Aptness of language** – do your chosen words convey your intended meaning?
- **Sentence length** – is there enough variety, with the occasional longer or shorter sentence thrown in to add pace and interest?
- **Overall length** – can anything be pruned to aid brevity?

Spot errors and inelegancies. Correct them. Reword stilted sentences and sections so that they flow. Invert the word order in some sentences to avoid monotony and add interest. Looking back at the running shoe example, the writer may decide on reflection that the Hi-star credentials section is unnecessary: the company has been in business for 50 years and top runners already wear its shoes. By

> **tip**
>
> Complete as many revisions as necessary, until you are happy with the result. Now it's time for a test drive. Ask for feedback from some guinea pigs. Don't pick your mother/best friend: they will tell you your work is wonderful! Select people from your target audience. Listen carefully to the comments of your test-readers. If they don't understand something, find it boring, ill-organised or confusing, discuss what they would like to see. Take on board what you believe to be reasonable.

re-reading your work after an acceptable interval, you will be more objective, more critical and more refreshed.

Starting over

What if you hate the result? Start all over again. Although it can be utterly demoralising, never be afraid to bin your work. It is pointless struggling to make something of work that is meritless. Often a fresh start is easier, and the end product better, than a rehash. The more you write, the less often this will happen. But before you scrap your work, analyse it. What bits do you like? Are there particular words, phrases or sections that you are pleased with? Retain them and see if they can be reused. What do you dislike? Try to avoid this in the next draft.

Writer's block remedies

Even seasoned copywriters sometimes suffer from writer's block. Publisher-turned-author Michael Legat has written widely on how to write and get published. He says of writer's block, in his book *Writing For Pleasure and Profit*: 'I have little sympathy . . . writer's block has become a fashionable ailment, and it is certainly easier and more impressive to say that you are affected with it than that you are lazy.' There is some truth in this, but Legat's view is a tad harsh.

We've all been there. Sitting at your word processor, you gaze at the blank screen. The words just won't come. No inspiration can be found. Anything you manage to write is rubbish. Depression sets in. The mind begins to wander. You contemplate what to wear for Jamie's party, or what to cook when the Singhs come to dinner. Efforts to focus on the task are futile. Yes, I am talking from heartfelt experience! Writer's block did afflict me during the writing of this book! When writer's block sets in as hard as concrete, no good will come of forcing yourself to remain at your desk. But don't despair: there are techniques for getting started again when writer's block strikes:

Top tips for unblocking your mind

- **Turn out trash** – Write what you can, however dreadful, until the words begin to flow again. The important thing is to start writing: you can go back later and polish it. Once you've got something on paper, at least you are in a position to edit or redraft.
- **Alter assignment** – Try tackling a different assignment to see if it helps. You could even write about your writer's block!
- **Basic bodilies** – Hungry or tired writers are never at their best. Feeling zonked? Put off your writing to another day if possible. If you must press on, rest your head on your desk, eyes closed, for 15 minutes. It *will* help. Hungry? Get something to eat and the blood sugar surge will give your brain a boost.
- **Start simple** – Kick off with the easy bit of your copy – an order form, contact details or some other part that is undemanding. At least you are achieving something. Move on to tackle a slightly harder bit of text, and so on. Eventually you'll be back in full swing.
- **Down a dram** – Some writers swear that alcohol oils their creativity; others blame it for ruining their careers. When working at home, perhaps a *small* glass of wine (not a bottle!) will help you get started, though it might raise a few eyebrows in the office.
- **Coffee and cake** – If you've tried without success, take a break. Nip out for coffee and cake, and mull over your writing assignment. In the more relaxed atmosphere of a cafe, that elusive idea on which your copy will hang might come to you.
- **Dictate it** – Try saying what you want to write. Talk to a tape recorder or a real person. You're less likely to be lost for words when speaking than writing. Talking out loud can help get you going.
- **Adrenaline action** – Go for a bracing walk or a quick jog round the block, then use the resultant adrenaline rush to recharge your grey matter.
- **Alternative activity** – Try doing something else for a while. Make a few phone calls, catch up on some reading or go through your in-tray. But don't waste the day: after a reasonable interval, make sure you get back to your writing.

TRUE STORY

Best-selling author Dan Brown, who wrote *The Da Vinci Code*, takes a break from writing every hour to do press-ups.

Physical exercise is a good stimulant for the creative juices.

- **Schedule an early session** – The human brain is at its best in the morning. If you face a difficult writing assignment, do it first thing, while you are fresh and your brain is in prime form.
- **Take a break** – Experts suggest that you take a short (perhaps five-minute) break after 45 minutes, to restore concentration.
- **Avoid afternoons** – Mental decline sets in at about 4pm so avoid this slot if you can. Starting to write at this time will be harder and writer's block more likely.
- **Word warm-ups** – Play a few word games or do a crossword to warm up your brain ready for writing. You could even have a go at some of the exercises in Chapter 9.
- **Reach for inspiration** – Look at other people's adverts, brochures, leaflets and newsletters. See if you can find inspiration from their work.
- **Consult colleagues** – Writing is a solitary business. Getting nowhere fast? Talk it over with colleagues. See if they can provide you with a different insight, a new angle or an enlightened thought.
- **Brainstorm** – Jot down anything related to what you are writing about: quotes, key words, adjectives. It might just provide a catalyst to get you started.
- **Dish out discipline** – Sometimes writer's block is the result of laziness or lack of application. At such times, you will just have to force yourself to get on with it. Quit the delaying tactics (tidying your desk, making a cup of tea), admit that you are being lazy, and then settle down to work. Your writing assignment will not go away, so you've no choice. Get everything you need (paper, refreshments, notes . . .) so there's no excuse for leaving your desk. Such excuses merely break your concentration and make it even harder to get down to it.
- **More understanding** – Often there is a deep-seated reason for chronic writer's block. It may be to do with fear of failure. Analyse why you find writing so hard, then do something about it. It can be difficult to find the motivation for a dull or boring assignment. Inevitably not everything will fill you with enthusiasm. Much 'bread and butter' copywriting can be dreary. The more of it you have to do, the more depressing it becomes. When your heart sinks at the prospect of yet another unchallenging project, take heart. It's normal to feel this way. Park your despair, adopt an ultra-professional attitude, knuckle down and get the job completed to your usual high standards.
- **Writing rewards** – Give yourself a small treat (chocolate works well!) for every page you write, or every hour you work.
- **Personal pressure** – Put yourself under a little pressure. Even if there's no external pressure on you to finish the job, set a deadline and stick to it.

- **Diary a date** – Decide when you are going to do your writing, put it in your diary and block off the time.
- **Amphetamine action** – When the above remedies fail, an impending deadline will get you moving again. If you've got to do it, somehow you will! A leading copywriter described deadlines as: 'the legal amphetamines of copywriters, a little time pressure acting as a most effective stimulant'. He's right!

Writing that packs a punch

This chapter looks at simple but effective ways to guarantee that your copy packs a punch. Find out how to use plain English. Learn how to paint vivid pictures with words. Discover how the 'first person' makes your copy more personal. Pick up tips on how to create bite-size chunks.

You can spot the work of a good professional copywriter in an instant. It stands out, it demands to be read, it is sharp and snappy. How do the pros give their work these qualities? They use simple techniques to ensure their words have impact. Employ their trade secrets to instantly improve your copy.

First person

Make marketing material livelier by using the 'first person' to give your copy an instant lift. Inexperienced copywriters tend to write in the 'third person':

☒ *The Spingate Shopping Centre offers customers top name shops, free parking and a free shuttle bus from the town centre. Shoppers will find that the Spingate provides everything the High Street can, and more besides.*

The third person makes copy impersonal, remote and distant. Use the first person as much as you can. It's much more intimate, more one-to-one, and more direct.

☑ *At the Spingate Shopping Centre you'll find top name shops, free parking and a free shuttle bus from the town centre. We provide everything the High Street can, and more besides.*

First person	The speaker (or writer)	I, we, me, us, my, mine, our, ours
Second person	The addressee (the person spoken to or the reader)	You, your, yours
Third person	A third party (the person or thing spoken about)	He/she, him/her, they/them, it, the charity, the company, their, theirs

Don't be afraid of words like 'we' and 'you'. They are preferable to circuitous abstractions such as 'the customer', 'the donor' and 'the purchaser'. When talking to a real, living, breathing person, don't dehumanise them by using the third person. You would never do it face-to-face. I have used the first person throughout this book – this sentence is a good example – enabling me to talk direct to you. Do the same with your readers.

Don't tell – show

Wannabe novelists are warned never to write a pedestrian account of what is happening. They learn to show the action through lively, active and descriptive language. The hallmark of effective copy, like a gripping novel, is text that shows, not tells. Take your reader with you. Make them feel involved, part of the action and not just a spectator. Show visually, by using a photograph, or paint a picture with words.

> ☒ *Slimline 100 is a simple, inexpensive and revolutionary weight loss programme to help you shed pounds fast. It has helped many users achieve dramatic weight loss with little effort or willpower.*

On the surface, this seems to be an acceptable piece of writing which states the facts clearly and persuasively. But it fails to conjure up a real picture that involves the reader: it is just telling. Here's how you show it:

> ☑ *Last year Mary weighed in at a hefty 18 stone. Today she's a slinky, sexy size 10. You too can achieve easy yet dramatic weight loss with Slimline 100. Picture yourself turning heads in skin-tight dresses, short skirts or skimpy bikinis. Make that dream a reality with Slimline 100.*

By showing, you are not simply listing what the product can do; you are demonstrating it in a powerful and personal way that involves the reader and offers a taste of what it can do for them.

Another way to show is to quantify by creating a mental image that people can relate to. To demonstrate the impact of traffic on the environment, you could write: 'Lorries of the nine major supermarkets travel a total of 670 million miles per year.' That would simply be telling. Show it by adding: 'That's equivalent to four return trips to the moon every day'. Now you're showing! You have created an image in the reader's mind that helps them understand just how great a distance 670 million miles is. To convey the magnitude of the nuclear waste storage problem, you could simply state how many tons of waste there will be nationwide after decommissioning. That would be telling. Or you could show it by explaining that it would be enough to fill the Albert Hall five times over. Now the readers can relate to what you are saying.

Consider using photos to reinforce the picture you painted with words. When American TV presenter Oprah Winfrey lost nearly five stone, she demonstrated the enormity of her weight loss using a supermarket trolley laden with 67lbs of lard. That's a brilliant illustration of how it is better to show than tell. Supermarket chain Sainsbury's used the same trick to show the superiority of their reward card. Full-page newspaper adverts showed two photographs. One was a trolley piled high with scores of jars of coffee, captioned: 'To get 300 points with the other supermarkets' cards'. The second photo showed a supermarket trolley with just three jars of coffee in it, captioned: 'To get 300 points with your Sainsbury's Reward Card.'

Contractions

Give vitality to your writing by mimicking the spoken word. Never be afraid to contract where appropriate: 'I've' instead of 'I have', for example. A few people regard contractions as unacceptable in written English. Let them. Most of us prefer to read copy that flows, and contractions do aid flow, making text more chatty, informal, friendly and readable. You'll see (as in this sentence) that I've used this technique to give this book a less stuffy feel.

This advice may be at odds with what you had drummed into you at school. So what? Copywriting is not the same as writing an essay or a school project (or even a business report). Creative copywriting breaks the rules. What might offend the grammatical purists may be perfect fodder for copywriters. Be led by what feels and sounds right, but be careful not to overdo it.

Situational copy

Sometimes copy takes on more meaning and relevance if you can link it to where it is being heard or read. Imagine you have just tucked into a slap-up meal. The waiter hands you your bill, on which is printed:

☑ *We don't want to take you on a guilt trip, but in the time it took you to eat your meal, 200 children died of starvation in the Third World. The cost of your dinner would be enough to feed all of them. Please donate to War on Famine.*

The above fictitious approach is a bit (too?) hard-hitting, but it makes the point. It links your experience (the meal you have eaten) with a fact that is in reality totally unrelated (the 200 children who have died). By linking them, it passes on a sense of responsibility to you that you might otherwise have been able to deny.

☒ *Every hour, 200 children die of starvation. Just £25 could feed all of them for a day. Please donate to War on Famine.*

As this example does not connect with your immediate experience, it is easy to ignore.

The following real life examples (from ads on the London Underground) illustrate situational copy, albeit in a less extreme way:

Victoria Line trains will be running frequently today. Without Nurofen Cold and Flu alas so will your nose

Easier on the tubes
[ad for a soft paper handkerchief]

[drawing of man and woman passing on different escalators in the Underground]

Don't let love pass you by. The person you go past or the person sitting next to you could be your future partner

[ad for a dating agency]

The copy is appropriate to the situation of the adverts on the Underground. So is this (for headache powders, displayed inside a bus):

Just the ticket for a headache

It's not startlingly clever, but it still links to the situation. People reading it will be clutching their bus tickets, so the link exists, however tenuously. The same product is also advertised on bus exteriors:

Gets to work faster than this bus

Words with personality

Listening to someone speak it's easy to get a feel for their personality, whether it is bubbly, shy, businesslike, friendly . . . or whatever. The written word can also convey personality. You can spot writers who are grovelling, arrogant, obsequious, helpful, and a hundred other personality types. Adopt a fitting personality for each assignment. Knowing how you want to come across will help you write in the appropriate style and to select an apt vocabulary.

Plain English

The best copy is written in plain English. Pick up any tabloid newspaper. The content might not be to your taste, but the copy is eminently readable. You can spring through it with ease. There's no stumbling on difficult words or grappling with long and complex paragraphs. Even upmarket copy should emulate this easy-read style.

Hutchinson's Concise Dictionary of English Usage says that plain English is: 'clear, concise, effective, interesting English. It saves time, paper, and misunderstanding, and so it saves money . . . Research shows that simple language sells products and services better than any other kind.' These are powerful reasons why you should adopt plain English as your language of choice.

Plain English is much misunderstood. It's not about patronising, over-simplified, 'dumbed down', 'Janet-and-John' style writing. It's simply about making your copy accessible and easy to read.

DOS AND DON'TS OF PLAIN ENGLISH

DO

☑ Use short words.

☑ Use fairly short sentences (15–20 words).

☑ Use the first person.

☑ Follow a clear and logical order.

☑ Show an understanding of what the reader needs to know.

DON'T

☒ Use jargon (unless it will be understood) or unnecessary technical terms.

☒ Use legalese or officialese.

☒ Use the passive voice (see next section).

☒ Pad – say what you have to say and then stop!

---

tip

Sometimes copy requires tact. It's best to refer to your cheap hotel as 'budget-priced'. Calling a spade a spade can be counterproductive if it forces your customers to acknowledge an unpalatable truth: that they are broke/bald/smelly/ugly. Make them feel good about the purchase, not miserable.

tip

Think of jargon as a foreign language. There's no point in talking to someone in Italian if they only understand French. Jargon is perfectly legitimate and extremely useful – if understood by both writer and reader. But as a rule, try not to be a jargonaut.

To find out more about plain English, get in touch with the Plain English Campaign (PO Box 3, New Mills, Stockport, SK12 4QP. Tel. 01663 744409 www.plainenglish.co.uk). They produce an *A – Z Guide of Alternative Words* and a pack on how to write letters in plain English, and they run courses. They also operate the 'Crystal Mark', a symbol you can display on your material (subject to approval by the Campaign, and payment of the appropriate fee) as a sign that your writing is clear and gobbledegook-free.

Also contact the Plain Language Commission (The Castle, 29 Stoneheads, Whaley Bridge, Stockport SK12 7BB. Tel. 01663 733177 www.clearest.co.uk) which was established by Martin Cutts, co-founder of the Plain English Campaign. They can advise on the readability of copy and offer advice to ensure your design aids clarity. The Plain Language Commission offers a kitemark, the 'Clear English Standard', which works in a similar way to the Plain English Campaign's symbol.

Keep active

As you will remember from school, verbs are 'doing words' such as 'hit' and 'feel'. There are 'active' verbs and 'passive' verbs. Powerful publicity uses the 'active voice'.

☒ *The best furniture in town is **sold** by us*
[passive]

☑ *We **sell** the best furniture in town*
[active]

You are saying the same thing in both these examples, but the second one is more succinct and has more punch. Use the 'active' voice to make your copy clearer, more direct, more personal – and shorter! The 'passive' voice is harder to read and understand, not to mention longer!

The active voice is where someone does something:

Jane kissed Sanjiv.
[3 words]

The early bird catches the worm.
[6 words]

The passive voice is where something is done to someone:

Sanjiv was kissed by Jane.
[5 words]

The worm is caught by the early bird.
[8 words]

The word order for active is:

1. Subject (Jane, the doer).
2. Verb (to kiss, a doing word).
3. Object (Sanjiv).

For passive sentences, it's the reverse: object, verb, subject.

Bite-sized chunks

Acres of unbroken copy overwhelm and are a guaranteed turn-off. The mere sight of great slabs of text is enough to deter even the most determined reader. What matters is not how long your copy is, but how long your reader *thinks* it is. One page of unbroken copy is more difficult to read than two pages of bite-size chunks. Tricks for converting long screeds of text into readable and easily digestible chunks include:

Bulletpoints

Don't overlook the humble bulletpoint. It offers a wonderfully simple yet effective way of presenting what would otherwise be a rather daunting list.

☒ *In all Heritage hotels you will find: an indoor heated swimming pool, jacuzzi, sauna and steam room; a fully equipped gym with cardio equipment and weights; plush rooms with satellite TV, minibar, wifi internet access and trouser press; a cocktail bar, coffee shop and gourmet restaurant; business facilities, meeting rooms and secretarial services; mini cinema and shopping mall; free parking and free shuttle bus to the airport.*

☑ *In all Heritage hotels you will find:*

- *An indoor heated swimming pool, jacuzzi, sauna and steam room.*
- *A fully equipped gym with cardio equipment and weights.*
- *Plush rooms with satellite TV, minibar, wifi internet access and trouser press.*
- *A cocktail bar, coffee shop and gourmet restaurant.*
- *Business facilities, meeting rooms and secretarial services.*
- *Mini cinema and shopping mall.*
- *Free parking and free shuttle bus to the airport.*

The bulletpointed list is less overwhelming, and it gives each of the items in the list more prominence.

Callouts/pull quotes

A callout or pull quote is a useful device both for breaking up text and for drawing attention to a particularly important section of copy. Here's an example:

Garavelli's: Bringing the Mediterranean to Britain

Garavelli's terracotta pots are hand-made in the traditional way in a string of picturesque Tuscan villages. Each pot is individually thrown, shaped and decorated, then fired at high temperatures to make it frost-proof, essential for our chillier climes. No two pots are the same, unlike the mass produced containers available in garden centres.

Each pot is individually thrown, shaped and decorated, then fired at high temperatures to make it frost-proof, essential for our chillier climes.

Every Garavelli planter has its own personality and each bears the signature of the maker.

Bring the warmth and colour of Tuscany to your own garden with a Garavelli hand-crafted terracotta pot. Available only by mail order, direct from Garavelli's. Call for a brochure. Prices start at just £9.99 for a 12-inch pot.

The callout breaks up the text, while simultaneously highlighting a key section of copy. It is a device that can be used in leaflets, brochures, adverts and newsletter articles.

Boxes

Consider creating a bite-size chunk by 'boxing off' a section. Like a callout, a box can both break up text and draw attention to the passage selected for boxing. On the next page, you can see a fictitious newsletter article featuring dense, unbroken text. On the following page the use of boxes transforms identical text into a more readable and lively page. When you write long copy, look out for anything that can be boxed.

Indian food with a difference

Vegetarians in Anyville can now enjoy gourmet Indian food, thanks to the opening of Rajah's, the town's latest restaurant. Although not exclusively vegetarian (it has a small selection of chicken and fish dishes), Rajah's has an extensive and impressive vegetarian menu, with a number of vegan dishes.

Rajah's is quite unlike other Indian restaurants. There's no flock wallpaper to be seen, no paper tablecloths or plastic flowers. The elegant decor includes handmade tiles specially commissioned in India, imported rosewood tables and chairs, original Indian art, and handprinted table linen adorned with Rajah's distinctive paisley logo.

The emphasis is on fine food prepared in a traditional manner. While Rajah's kitchen is brand new, many of the utensils are the same as those used in India hundreds of years ago. The chefs believe that the use of original cooking implements creates a more authentic taste and texture. Each dish leaving Rajah's kitchen is guaranteed to be free from colourings, additives and preservatives.

The owners of Rajah's made a 10,000-mile round trip to recruit its chefs, one from the north of India and the other from the south. They bring with them specialist knowledge of a wide range of regional dishes, such as the rich, sweetly spiced main courses from the south, featuring nuts, coconut milk and lemon, as well as the more familiar northern Indian food, such as matar paneer, a dish made with peas and cubes of tofu-like home-made cottage cheese.

Vegetarians can choose from 11 starters, 20 main courses, seven side dishes, seven types of rice, and 11 types of bread. The first courses are impressively varied, ranging from bhelpuris (a Mumbai roadside snack of puffed rice, crushed potatoes and tamarind sauce) to dal vada, crispy dumplings made with crushed chickpeas, yellow lentils and onions. You'll also find more familiar starters, such as samosa and pakora.

The main courses, too numerous to mention, are split into north Indian cuisine, south Indian dishes, and 'thalis'. A thali is a large plate, on which are assembled a number of smaller dishes, rather like a meze. There is a north and a south Indian thali, a special Rajah's thali, and a vegan one.

Anyone for pudding? Rajah's offers the usual range of desserts (kulfi, halwa and gulab jamun) as well as some unusual and mouth-watering concoctions, such as shrikhand, a golden yoghurt dessert garnished with saffron and pistachio, or kheer, a pudding made with rice, nuts, raisins and saffron.

There are even Indian drinks. Lassi is a delicious yoghurt drink, and Rajah's serve it in several varieties, including mango flavour, namkeen lassi (salty and subtly spiced) and meethi lassi, which is sweet, smooth and thirst-quenching. There's also south Indian coffee on the menu, Indian tea, and herbal tea.

So if you fancy an Indian meal with a difference, try Rajah's. And if you're really lucky, you might choose a night when Indian classical musicians are performing.

Indian food with a difference

Vegetarians in Anyville can now enjoy gourmet Indian food, thanks to the opening of Rajah's, the town's latest restaurant. Although not exclusively vegetarian (it has a small selection of chicken and fish dishes), Rajah's has an extensive and impressive vegetarian menu, with a number of vegan dishes.

Rajah's is quite unlike other Indian restaurants. There's no flock wallpaper to be seen, no paper tablecloths or plastic flowers. The elegant decor includes handmade tiles specially commissioned in India, imported rosewood tables and chairs, original Indian art, and handprinted table linen adorned with Rajah's distinctive paisley logo.

The emphasis is on fine food prepared in a traditional manner. While Rajah's kitchen is brand new, many of the utensils are the same as those used in India hundreds of years ago. The chefs believe that the use of original cooking implements creates a more authentic taste and texture. Each dish leaving Rajah's kitchen is guaranteed to be free from colourings, additives and preservatives.

MORE CHOICE

Vegetarians can choose from:

- 11 starters
- 20 main courses
- seven side dishes
- seven types of rice
- 11 types of bread

The owners of Rajah's made a 10,000-mile round trip to recruit its chefs, one from the north of India and the other from the south. They bring with them specialist knowledge of a wide range of regional dishes, such as the rich, sweetly spiced main courses from the south, featuring nuts, coconut milk and lemon, as well as the more familiar northern Indian food, such as matar paneer, a dish made with peas and cubes of tofu-like home-made cottage cheese.

ANYONE FOR PUDDING?

Rajah's offers the usual range of desserts (kulfi, halwa and gulab jamun) as well as some unusual and mouth-watering concoctions, such as shrikhand, a golden yoghurt dessert garnished with saffron and pistachio, or kheer, a pudding made with rice, nuts, raisins and saffron.

The first courses are impressively varied, ranging from bhelpuris (a Mumbai roadside snack of puffed rice, crushed potatoes and tamarind sauce) to dal vada, crispy dumplings made with crushed chickpeas, yellow lentils and onions. You'll also find more familiar starters, such as samosa and pakora.

The main courses, too numerous to mention, are split into north Indian cuisine, south Indian dishes, and 'thalis'. A thali is a large plate, on which are assembled a number of smaller dishes, rather like a meze. There is a north and a south Indian thali, a special Rajah's thali, and a vegan one.

There are even Indian drinks. Lassi is a delicious yoghurt drink, and Rajah's serve it in several varieties, including mango flavour, namkeen lassi (salty and subtly spiced) and meethi lassi, which is sweet, smooth and thirst-quenching. There's also south Indian coffee on the menu, Indian tea, and herbal tea.

So if you fancy an Indian meal with a difference, try Rajah's. And if you're really lucky, you might choose a night when Indian classical musicians are performing.

---

tip

You will notice that numbers one to ten in the 'Indian Food With a Difference' article are spelt out, whereas numbers from 11 upwards are presented as numerics. This is a standard publishing house style. Use it to make your copy look professional and to ensure consistency in how numbers are presented in text. For other ideas on house style, consult one of the online newspaper style guides.

Subheadings

This common device is surprisingly neglected. Interesting sub-headings break up text, signpost the reader and entice them to read on. The Indian restaurant feature appears much more readable with subheadings:

Indian food with a difference

Vegetarians in Anyville can now enjoy gourmet Indian food, thanks to the opening of Rajah's, the town's latest restaurant. Although not exclusively vegetarian (it has a small selection of chicken and fish dishes), Rajah's has an extensive and impressive vegetarian menu, with a number of vegan dishes.

No flock wallpaper!

Rajah's is quite unlike other Indian restaurants. There's no flock wallpaper to be seen, no paper tablecloths or plastic flowers. The elegant decor includes handmade tiles specially commissioned in India, imported rosewood tables and chairs, original Indian art, and handprinted table linen adorned with Rajah's distinctive paisley logo.

The emphasis is on fine food prepared in a traditional manner. While Rajah's kitchen is brand new, many of the utensils are the same as those used in India hundreds of years ago. The chefs believe that the use of original cooking implements creates a more authentic taste and texture. Each dish leaving Rajah's kitchen is guaranteed to be free from colourings, additives and preservatives.

10,000-mile trip to recruit chefs

The owners of Rajah's made a 10,000-mile round trip to recruit its chefs, one from the north of India and the other from the south. They bring with them specialist knowledge of a wide range of regional dishes, such as the rich, sweetly spiced main courses from the south, featuring nuts, coconut milk and lemon, as well as the more familiar northern Indian food, such as matar paneer, a dish made with peas and cubes of tofu-like home-made cottage cheese.

Mumbai roadside snacks

Vegetarians can choose from 11 starters, 20 main courses, seven side dishes, seven types of rice, and 11 types of bread. The first courses are impressively varied, ranging from bhelpuris (a Mumbai roadside snack of puffed rice, crushed potatoes and tamarind sauce) to dal vada, crispy dumplings made with crushed chickpeas, yellow lentils and onions. You'll also find more familiar starters, such as samosa and pakora.

The main courses, too numerous to mention, are split into north Indian cuisine, south Indian dishes, and 'thalis'. A thali is a large plate, on which are assembled a number of smaller dishes, rather like a meze. There is a north and a south Indian thali, a special Rajah's thali, and a vegan one.

Anyone for pudding? Rajah's offers the usual range of desserts (kulfi, halwa and gulab jamun) as well as some unusual and mouth-watering concoctions, such as shrikhand, a golden yoghurt dessert garnished with saffron and pistachio, or kheer, a pudding made with rice, nuts, raisins and saffron.

Indian classical music

There are even Indian drinks. Lassi is a delicious yoghurt drink, and Rajah's serve it in several varieties, including mango flavour, namkeen lassi (salty and subtly spiced) and meethi lassi, which is sweet, smooth and thirst-quenching. There's also south Indian coffee on the menu, Indian tea, and herbal tea.

So if you fancy an Indian meal with a difference, try Rajah's. And if you're really lucky, you might choose a night when Indian classical musicians are performing.

Combine all these copy-breaking devices – bulletpoints, callouts, boxes and subheadings – to create copy that appears less daunting and more readable. Compare the following with the original version on page 39. I know which I'd rather read!

Indian food with a difference

Vegetarians in Anyville can now enjoy gourmet Indian food, thanks to the opening of Rajah's, the town's latest restaurant. Although not exclusively vegetarian (it has a small selection of chicken and fish dishes), Rajah's has an extensive and impressive vegetarian menu, with a number of vegan dishes.

No flock wallpaper!

Rajah's is quite unlike other Indian restaurants. There's no flock wallpaper to be seen, no paper tablecloths or plastic flowers. The elegant decor includes handmade tiles specially commissioned in India, imported rosewood tables and chairs, original Indian art, and handprinted table linen adorned with Rajah's distinctive paisley logo.

The emphasis is on fine food prepared in a traditional manner. While Rajah's kitchen is brand new, many of the utensils are the same as those used in India hundreds of years ago. The chefs believe that the use of original cooking implements creates a more authentic taste and texture. Each dish leaving Rajah's kitchen is guaranteed to be free from colourings, additives and preservatives.

> While Rajah's kitchen is brand new, many of the utensils are the same as those used by Indians hundreds of years ago . . . Each dish leaving Rajah's kitchen is guaranteed to be free from colourings, additives and preservatives.

10,000-mile trip to recruit chefs

The owners of Rajah's made a 10,000-mile round trip to recruit its chefs, one from the north of India and the other from the south. They bring with them specialist knowledge of a wide range of regional dishes, such as the rich, sweetly spiced main courses from the south, which feature nuts, coconut milk and lemon, as well as the more familiar northern Indian food, such as matar paneer, a dish made with peas and cubes of tofu-like home-made cottage cheese.

MORE CHOICE

Vegetarians can choose from:

- 11 starters
- 20 main courses
- seven side dishes
- seven types of rice
- 11 types of bread

Mumbai roadside snacks

The first courses are impressively varied, ranging from bhelpuris (a Mumbai roadside snack of puffed rice, crushed potatoes and tamarind sauce) to dal vada, crispy dumplings made with crushed chickpeas, yellow lentils and onions. You'll also find more familiar starters, such as samosa and pakora.

The main courses, too numerous to mention, are split into north Indian cuisine, south Indian dishes, and 'thalis'. A thali is a large plate, on which are assembled a number of smaller dishes, rather like a meze. There is a north and a south Indian thali, a special Rajah's thali, and a vegan one.

Anyone for pudding? Rajah's offers the usual range of desserts (kulfi, halwa and gulab jamun) as well as some unusual and mouth-watering concoctions, such as shrikhand, a golden yoghurt dessert garnished with saffron and pistachio, or kheer, a pudding made with rice, nuts, raisins and saffron.

Indian classical music

There are even Indian drinks. Lassi is a delicious yoghurt drink, and Rajah's serve it in several varieties, including mango flavour, namkeen lassi (salty and subtly spiced) and meethi lassi, which is sweet, smooth and thirst-quenching. There's also south Indian coffee on the menu, Indian tea, and herbal tea.

So if you fancy an Indian meal with a difference, try Rajah's. And if you're really lucky, you might choose a night when Indian classical musicians are performing.

The dreaded grammar and English

If grammar fills you with fear, this chapter is for you. Discover the most common grammatical mistakes and how to avoid them. Learn how to restructure your sentences to make them livelier. Find out how to remove bias from your writing.

It would be too much to hope that a book on writing could avoid the subject of grammar altogether. Correct grammar is essential for effective copy. But don't worry. You don't need to learn about all of the terrifying complexities of grammar because, whether you know it or not, you already have an instinctive feel for correct usage. As long as your grammar is correct, does it really matter whether you understand *why* it is right? You don't need to know a 'past participle' from a 'conjunction', so long as you know how to use them. We all know that 'I are no good at grammar, is I?' is ungrammatical, even though we might struggle to explain why.

TRUE STORY

A factor making human language unique is 'recursion' – our ability to insert a clause into a sentence so that it still makes sense. Scientists have established that starlings are able to grasp complex grammatical rules and to recognise recursion. Pretty impressive, as even monkeys cannot do that!

You follow the principal rules of English usage already, so it's the everyday grammatical errors that we need to concentrate on, beginning with the most common mistakes.

Common grammatical mistakes

Commas for full stops or colons

People frequently use commas where they should use full stops, making their writing harder to follow. Remember, the harder it is to read and make sense of, the less likely it is to be read at all. Here's an example from a printed sign above the doorway of my local pizza parlour:

☒ *Welcome to Pizza Italy, please wait to be seated.*

A comma separates two completely discrete sentences, making two distinct points. As we all know, sentences are separated by full stops. Here another typical example:

☒ *Place your order now, this offer expires at the end of the month.*

☑ *Place your order now, as this offer expires at the end of the month.*

☑ *Place your order now. This offer expires at the end of the month.*

When placing a comma, think: 'is a comma required here, or have I reached the end of the sentence?'. Sometimes you might feel that a comma would be wrong, but a full stop would be too final. In such cases, the colon is useful. As in this example:

☑ *Place your order now: this offer expires at the end of the month.*

Singulars for plurals

It is not uncommon for people to take a singular noun and add a plural verb. You will often see:

☒ *There **are** a host of benefits attached to this deal . . .*

As 'host' is singular, it should read:

☑ *There **is** a host of . . .*

Another example:

☒ *You'll be spoilt for choice, as there **are** plenty to choose from*

☑ *You'll be spoilt for choice, as there **is** plenty to choose from*

Always check that your noun and verb agree.

Wrong use of initial capitals

Much marketing copy is spoiled by an over generous helping of wrongly applied initial capitals. An initial capital is a capital letter at the start of a word. Only use one when:

- the word is a proper noun (Birmingham, Ellie);
- the word is a company name (Marks and Spencer, Waterstone's);
- the word is the first in a sentence.

All too often, you see this:

☒ *Farmer Foods promise You the very Best Choice and Value for fresh vegetables, Frozen meals and Dairy produce.*

Don't litter your prose with initial capitals. This kind of usage is incorrect, ugly and distracting.

☑ *Farmer Foods promise you the very best choice and value for fresh vegetables, frozen meals and dairy produce.*

Apostrophes

The phenomenon disparagingly referred to as the 'greengrocer's apostrophe,' sadly is not confined to greengrocers: it afflicts many a marketing copywriter. Call in at your nearest greengrocer to see it in action:

☒ *Pear's 75p   Apple's 60p   Grape's £1*

You will frequently see this kind of thing:

☒ *Chumpley's Health Farm will get you fit. We have four sauna's, two gym's and ten exercise bike's. There's even a childrens' gym. And every night we run a 60's disco.*

In case you're not sure, this is how it should be:

☑ *Chumpley's Health Farm will get you fit. We have four saunas, two gyms and ten exercise bikes. There's even a children's gym. And every night we run a '60s disco.*

- **Saunas** – The plural of sauna is saunas, not sauna's. Some people erroneously believe that if a word ends with a vowel (cameras, logos, taxis), the plural requires an apostrophe in order to aid pronunciation. Without the help of an apostrophe, they think 'cameras' would be pronounced 'camer-ass' and 'logos' 'log-oss'. They are wrong!

- **'60s** – This is short for the 1960s. Therefore, the apostrophe goes before the '60' to denote that the '19' has been dropped.
- **Gyms/bikes** – These are simply plurals so they do not need an apostrophe 's'.
- **Children's** – This should have an apostrophe because it is a possessive: a gym for children. Normally with a possessive plural, the apostrophe comes *after* the 's' (the sisters' rabbit – a rabbit belonging to some sisters), but not always.

☑ *The boys' gym*
[more than one boy]

☑ *The boy's gym*
[one boy]

☑ *The man's gym*
[one man]

☑ *The men's gym*
[more than one man, but as 'men' is a plural which does not end in 's', you need to add an apostrophe followed by an 's' to turn it into a possessive plural]

☑ *The ladies' gym*
[more than one lady, but as 'ladies' is a plural which ends in 's', simply add an apostrophe after the 's', as you would with 'the sisters' rabbit']

The rules are simple. Use an apostrophe only:

- to denote possession: the company's policy; the shop's opening hours; Spike's guitar;
- to indicate that something has been omitted: '80s (1980s); shouldn't (should not); 'til (until).

Confusing it's/its

The rule is so simple. There's no excuse for confusing it's/its. 'It's' is a contraction for either 'it is' or 'it has':

It's (it has) been rather cold lately.
I had planned to walk, but it's (it is) just too far.

'Its' means something quite different. It means 'belonging to it':

'You'll love its taste.'
Where's its bone gone?

Best-selling writer Lynne Truss is unforgiving of people confusing the possessive 'its' with the contractive 'it's', stating that they deserve to be: 'struck down by lightening, hacked up on the spot and buried in an unmarked grave'. Harsh!

Confusion arises because people are taught to use an apostrophe to denote possession. As 'its' is a possessive pronoun, people understandably believe it should have an apostrophe. After all, we'd be correct in writing:

You'll love this chocolate's taste.
Where's the dog's bone gone?

However, the rule is that possessive pronouns (its, hers, ours, yours, theirs) should not have an apostrophe. The exception is 'one's' – 'One must always try one's best.'

There's further confusion with names ending in 's': James, Charles, Bridget Jones. Should you write 'Charles's wife' or Charles' wife'? As various punctuation guides disagree on this point, it's a matter of personal choice although there appears to be a preference for the extra 's' – 'Bridget Jones's diary'. The exception is when a name ends with 'es', creating an 'iz' sound, such as 'Moses' – here it would sound odd as 'Moses's tablets' (it needs to be 'Moses' tablets').

What about plural names ending in 's', such as 'Jones'? Something belonging to one Jones would be:

Mrs Jones' shop

Or, if you prefer:

Mrs Jones's shop

The plural of 'Jones' is 'Joneses', as in 'keeping up with the Joneses'. Therefore, something belonging to more than one Jones would be:

The Joneses' shop.

It's simple. Take the name (Jones) and pluralise it (Joneses) and then add the apostrophe in the correct place (after the 's', as it's a plural that ends in 's') to denote possession.

> **tip**
>
> Read self-confessed punctuation addict Lynne Truss's excellent and witty *Eats, Shoots & Leaves* if you're a stickler for the apostrophe in particular and punctuation in general.

> **tip**
>
> No apostrophe is needed to denote the plural of an acronym or abbreviation. Therefore, we would write: 'The PCs in my office are old and need to be replaced'. However, for a possessive acronym or abbreviation, an apostrophe is required to indicate possession: 'My PC's performance is not good because it is old and obsolete'. The apostrophe goes before the 's', as we are talking about one PC. For a plural possessive, it goes after the 's', as in: 'The office PCs' replacements arrive today'.

Misused inverted commas

Inverted commas are frequently misused. You will often see:

'Free'
☒ *A fantastic gift 'free' with every order. But Hurry! 'Limited offer'.*

Here inverted commas have been placed around words to emphasise and draw attention to them. But that's not the correct use of inverted commas. They should indicate that the writer is using the word in an unusual or ironic way:

☑ *The 'free' gift actually ended up costing me a fortune!*

The writer here is saying that the gift was anything but free. If you want to emphasise words, **do not** put inverted commas around them. Try using bold, underlining or using italics.

My husband and I

Frequently people write (and say) 'I' when it should be 'me':

☒ *This is a great opportunity for my husband and I to . . .*

This is wrong. But this is right:

☑ *My husband and I think this is a great opportunity to . . .*

Confused? It's simple really. Take the first example. You would never write:

☒ *This is a great opportunity for I . . .*

You would write:

☑ *This is a great opportunity for me . . .*

If you are not sure, try saying the sentence without the 'my husband' bit. If you would say 'I', say 'my husband and I'. If you would say 'me', say 'my husband and me'.

How good is your grammar?

That concludes the whistle-stop tour of grammar. It wasn't too painful, was it? Now for a quick test to see whether you understand the basics. Answer the following questions then check your score. If you get any wrong, make sure you understand why.

Grammar test

In each of the sentences below, consider whether the grammar is correct. If you believe it is right, tick it; if it's incorrect, mark it with a cross. If you think something is wrong, correct it.

1. The number of new customers we win each day are increasing rapidly.
2. All ladies' and boy's clothing is half price.
3. Less people took up this offer than I would have hoped.
4. My colleagues and I would like to thank you for your continued custom.
5. None of us have a crystal ball. If only we had!
6. This delay will not help my colleagues or I to get our mailshot out on time.
7. We offer six types of fresh herbs with every salad dressing.
8. Eileen's new office was really spacious.

Answers

1. ☒ It should read: '. . . **is** increasing rapidly'. 'The number' is singular, so the verb must be singular too.
2. ☒ It should read: '. . . and **boys'** clothing . . .' 'Boys' is a plural and therefore the apostrophe should come after the letter 's'.
3. ☒ It should read: '. . . **Fewer** people . . .' You can read more about less/fewer on page 53.
4. ☑
5. ☒ It should read: '. . . None of us **has** . . .' 'None' is singular, so the verb must agree.
6. ☒ It should read: '. . . will not help **me** or my colleagues . . .'
7. ☒ It should read: '. . . of fresh **herb** . . .'
8. ☑

How did you do? Got a few wrong? Learn from your mistakes. If you earned a full score, well done! Your grammar is in tiptop condition for the copywriting tasks ahead of you.

Now it's time to move to on to English, how we use it, and how we can improve our use of it.

English

Letters form words, words form sentences, and sentences form paragraphs. We all have access to the same 26 letters of the alphabet, and to the same huge vocabulary (there were 600,000 words in the *Oxford English Dictionary* at last count, but most of us typically use just 2000 of them!). Some of us are able to turn that raw material into

tip

Never accept the first word that springs to mind. Does your chosen word have any unpleasant or unwanted connotations? Is it the right word to use in this context? Will your reader understand it? Consider the alternatives. Are there better, more appropriate, shorter, more powerful or descriptive substitutes?

compelling, powerful and memorable material: others struggle just to make themselves understood. The way you use language sets your copy apart from less skilled wordsmiths, so it is worth spending a little time analysing words and sentences.

Words

Mark Twain said: 'Writing is easy. All you have to do is cross out the wrong words.' Someone else (I can't remember who) summed up poetry as the process of selecting the right words in the right order. It sure makes a complex creative process sound easy! Half a dozen well-chosen words *can* add up to a powerful marketing message, but which words? How do you choose the right ones? Which should you avoid? In what order do you string them together?

The fewer words you use, the more work they have to do. A writer will give as much thought to four words in a hoarding headline as 2,000 words in a brochure. Why? Those four words will have to do the same job as 2,000: they will need to sell. Four ill-chosen words will stand out like a beacon if the sum total of copy is just four words. But four inept words hiding among 2,000 are less noticeable.

There's no ready reckoner to show you which word to select, but there are some guiding principles for marketing copy:

- use short words;
- use familiar words;
- use spoken English;
- use 'concrete words';
- use powerful words;
- use confident words.

Short words

Opt for shorter words over longer ones, to make your copy easier to read. Choose 'use', not 'utilise'. Elect for 'live', not 'reside'. Two or three short words are better than one long one. Words of three or more syllables are harder to recognise and read.

Familiar words

Unfamiliar words interrupt the flow and cause readers to struggle. Replace unfamiliar and foreign words with everyday ones.

Spoken English

Many people who speak clearly and coherently become pompous and obscure when they write. Use words you would use if speaking. Write 'drink', not 'beverage', 'want', not 'desire'.

Concrete words

Some publicity material uses 'flowery' and vague language. Abstract words (wonderful, superb, fantastic, stylish) are over-used. Pin your copy down with plenty of concrete words that convey your meaning clearly, without leaving too much to individual interpretation. Here's a passage full of abstract words:

> ☒ *Our new range of wilton carpets will knock you sideways. Available in a wide choice of colours, each carpet is stylish and luxurious. Add its hardwearing qualities to its good looks and you'll have a carpet you simply can't beat. We're even offering some enticing credit deals into the bargain!*

This is much too general. What's stylish to a carpet retailer might be completely naff to the customer. The text is so unspecific that no clear picture is produced in the reader's head.

> ☑ *Our new range of wilton carpets comes in 24 colours, including plains and patterns (tartans, florals and abstract designs). Each carpet has a stain-repellent coating and comes with a ten-year guarantee. Who else offers such choice and interest-free credit?*

Now we're talking! This is clear and specific. It gives the facts, but presents them in an appealing way.

Powerful words

Research shows that certain words are highly effective at grabbing attention and thus are an excellent choice in publicity material.

- new
- free
- advice
- save
- money
- reduced
- how to
- announcing
- sex
- discovery
- now
- at last
- proven
- you.

They will not be effective for any and every use, and are not a quick and lazy alternative to well considered wording. Never simply string these magic words together – 'At last, announcing a proven way for you to save money!' – in the hope that you will get a result. It won't work! But used with care, these words are powerful in headlines (for adverts; in newsletters; and in direct mail, on envelopes and in the main and subheadings of mailshots).

Confident words

Be assertive and confident when you write.

☒ *We hope you will like your new . . . and hope you will want to take up our latest offer.*

☑ *We are confident you will like . . . and sure you will want to take up our latest offer.*

Stop qualifying everything you write; readers will pick up on insecurity. Have confidence in your products and services and let that confidence shine through in the words you select.

Commonly misused words

We all sometimes misuse words in everyday speech, but there's no excuse for copywriters doing this. The writer has the benefit of time to consider the choices and to select the appropriate word. Here are some commonly misused words, both in spoken and written English. Never be guilty of misusing them yourself:

Anticipating

Many people use this word when they actually mean 'expecting'. They may write: 'We anticipate that you will receive your order in the next week.' Anticipating requires some action to bring about a particular outcome. If you believe that you will get a record number

---

TRUE STORY

The longest word in any English dictionary is 'pneumonoultramicroscopicsilicovolcanoconiosis' (a lung disease caused by breathing in particles of silicous volcanic dust). Coined in 1935 by the President of The National Puzzlers' League, it was invented purely for the purpose of creating the longest word and is thus a bit of a cheat. Two chemical terms (3,641 and 1,913 letters long) appeared in the Guinness Book of World Records, but were withdrawn because chemists have never used them.

of orders, you could take on more staff to cope with the extra demand. You could then quite rightly claim to have anticipated the demand.

Presently

This does not mean that you are doing something now (in other words, currently); it means that you will do it shortly – 'We will presently be introducing our new season's range'.

Verbal

Too often this is used instead of 'oral'. Verbal involves words, which can be spoken or written. Oral refers purely to the spoken word.

Less/fewer

'Fewer' means 'not so many' while 'less' means 'not so much'. 'Less' is used when the number referred to is general; 'fewer' is used when the number refers to individual items.

> *There is less traffic on the motorway on a Sunday.*
> *There are fewer cars on the motorway on a Sunday.*

> *It is less crowded in the supermarket today.*
> *There are fewer people in the supermarket today.*

> *There is less choice in this dress shop than in the other one.*
> *There are fewer dresses in this shop than in the other one.*

Aggravate

This means 'to make worse'. If you scratch a spot, you will aggravate it. The word does not mean to irritate or annoy!

Imply/Infer

People infer (or deduce) things from what others have said or written. If someone hints at something, but does not say it directly, they are implying. The speaker (or writer) implies; the listener (or reader) infers.

Literally

How often do you hear people say absurd things like: 'The shops are literally on my doorstep' or 'He literally had me over a barrel'? The only things likely to be literally on your doorstep are visitors ringing your doorbell and bottles of milk! If you are literally over a barrel,

tip

A 27-word sentence is likely to be understood first time by just 4% of people. Or to put it another way, a sentence of that length will need to be reread by 96% of people if they are to understand it. Keep that fact in mind when you write.

then you must have a barrel beneath you, which is unlikely. And if you literally die laughing, you'll be literally six feet under!

Disinterested/uninterested

If you are disinterested, you are impartial or unbiased. Disinterested does *not* mean uninterested or indifferent. On the contrary, one is interested, but has no axe to grind.

Sentences

Well-structured sentences, comprising well-chosen words, create brilliant copy. But what makes a well-structured sentence? Do not look at sentences on their own; examine them together with their neighbours. For writing to have rhythm, look at sentence flow. While you should generally aim for fairly short sentences, vary the length here and there to avoid monotony. Longer ones add variety. So do very short ones. You can even use one-word sentences.

Inversion

A useful device for avoiding monotony is to invert the word order. Instead of following the usual word order and writing:

Many new products appear in this year's catalogue.

Invert it and write:

Appearing in this year's catalogue are many new products.

Rigidly following the usual word order, sentence after sentence, leads to dull, flat writing. Inversion can provide the necessary change of pace.

One-worders

We tend to think of sentences as comprising several words. One-word sentences are perfectly acceptable in publicity material and can add pace, drama and emphasis.

What's so different about the Wellington Cabriolet Gti? Well, it's nippy. Very. And fast. Really. In fact, it's in a class of its own.

This sentence would lack pace if it were rewritten to avoid one-word sentences. It's the staccato rhythm given by the one-worders that helps convey a meaning beyond the words. Here's another example of the technique in action:

It's a cold, dark night. Wet too. You are female. Alone. And your car has just broken down. How do you feel? Scared? Unsure what to do? No need to worry. For Motor Club members help is at hand . . .

One word, on its own, can have more impact than the same word lost in a longer sentence. See!

Sentence types

There are four sentence types:

- **Statements** – Such sentences assert facts: 'You cannot buy a more powerful computer'.
- **Commands** – These sentences tell you to do something: 'Visit our bargain basement today'.
- **Questions** – 'Ever wondered why we're Britain's favourite charity?'
- **Exclamations** – These are expressions of surprise: 'Hurry! Offer strictly limited'.

Generally in short marketing copy, such as ads, you will use commands. Such sentences tend to be more personal, more direct and snappier. In brochures and longer copy, you will use a mixture of sentence types.

Tenses

Generally, it is better to write in the present tense. It sounds more current and more confident.

☒ *We have helped thousands of small businesses nationwide to cut their stationery bills.*
[past tense]

That is not as punchy and newsy as:

☑ *We help thousands of small businesses nationwide to cut their stationery bills*
[present tense]

Better still is the more active:

Thousands of small businesses nationwide are cutting their stationery bills thanks to us

Now for a look at bias in language.

Inclusive language

Some people poke fun at all things 'PC' (politically correct). Laugh at your peril. Produce non-inclusive copy and you reduce the impact of your marketing material by offending part of your audience. Why take the risk? Write great copy without offending a soul by following these guidelines:

Gender

Avoid sexist language by following these pointers:

- Remember that females over 18 are women, not girls.
- Only use 'lady' if you would use 'gentleman' when writing about a male. Don't talk about 'lady drivers' and 'lady doctors' unless you would refer to 'gentlemen drivers' and 'gentleman doctors'.
- Avoid both male and female gender stereotypes in your writing and in the imagery you choose for your marketing material.
- Avoid language that excludes women. Don't use words or expressions like: 'The man in the street'; 'telephones manned by'; 'layman' and so forth.
- Don't write 'he/his/him' when you are writing about people in general. There are various techniques you can use to avoid gender-exclusive language:

  - Pluralise the sentence. Instead of writing: 'If a customer cannot collect the goods from our store, he can arrange to have them delivered' you could write: 'If customers cannot collect the goods from our store, they can arrange to have them delivered'.
  - Use 'they' and 'their' for the singular. You could write: 'If a customer cannot collect the goods from our store, they can arrange to have them delivered'.
  - Rewrite the sentence to avoid 'his' altogether: 'If you cannot collect the goods from our store, we will arrange to have them delivered' or: 'Anyone unable to collect goods from our store can have them delivered'.
  - Use 'his/hers' and 's/he'. This can be cumbersome, so use it only if none of the above work: 'If a customer cannot collect the goods from our store, s/he can arrange to have them delivered'.

Race

- Avoid using 'black' in a negative way: 'black day', 'blacken the name of' and so on.
- The expression 'welshing on a deal' is common, but can result in complaints from Welsh people.
- Avoid racial stereotypes. Asians don't only run corner shops; Jews and Scots are not mean.

> **tip**
>
> Use neutral terms whenever possible: chair (or chairperson), businesspeople and so on. Avoid feminine forms such as clerkess and manageress. They sound weaker than the neutral manager and clerk.

Age

Older people do not recognise the popular media stereotype which often portrays them as crabby crinklies. If you write about old people in a stereotyped way, you will lose customers. With an ageing population, and the growing importance of 'grey power', that's something you should take seriously.

TRUE STORY

A group of older people, angry at their representation on road signs (looking infirm, with walking sticks) started a campaign for more positive images of old people. They commissioned designs showing them on skateboards and doing other non-stereotypical activities.

Disability

Many people who have a disability dislike the label 'the disabled', which classifies them according to their disability. The term 'people with a disability' is preferred, as this recognises the person before their disability. Replace terms such as 'the blind' and 'the deaf' with 'blind people' and 'deaf people'. Obviously words such as 'cripple', 'handicapped' and 'wheelchair-bound' are offensive and should be ditched. Mental health discrimination is unacceptable too, so avoid words likely to cause offence, such as psycho and nutter.

TRUE STORY

A snazzy, stylish new wheelchair was launched in 2005 called The Spazz. Opinion was divided about whether or not this product name was offensive. Some people believed that the word 'spazz' should be reclaimed and given positive associations, while others were deeply offended. The launch grabbed lots of headlines, but why risk upsetting a large proportion of potential buyers with a name that many do find offensive?

CHAPTER

6

Time-tested copywriting devices

Pick up powerful techniques to ensure you get the best from your raw material: words. Draw upon proven methods for writing lively, winning, profitable copy time after time. Find out how to use puns, write powerful headlines, and make your copy more readable.

There's no magic formula for a great piece of copy. Two copywriters can use completely different techniques yet both come up with great words. Equally, you might use a tried and tested technique and produce lousy copy. Techniques help, but they are not guarantees. You still have to work at it. The more effort you put into your writing, the less effort your audience will need to put into reading it. Aim for copy that is so easy to read that it masks the sweat and toil that produced it. Ensure your writing captures the energy and ease of the spoken word, minus the ums and ahs.

Put effort into your writing, make use of the techniques described in this chapter, and avoid the mistakes highlighted in the next one. You'll soon be well on your way to producing writing worth reading.

Here are 10 techniques that will give your copy a bit of fizz.

tip

According to linguistic experts, the sounds made by temporarily stopping the air stream with your tongue or lips are best for alliteration. These are 'p', 'b', 'm', 'n', 't', 'd', 'k', and 'g'.

Alliteration

Alliteration is the use of similar sounds at the beginning of neighbouring words:

Murphy's Muffins are munchy and more-ish!

The best alliteration involves more than just the repeating of sounds. It is far more subtle and musical, ensuring that the words trip off the tongue.

Puns

One of the most common devices in marketing copy, the pun (or play on words) is especially good for headlines in adverts and articles. Puns can be a great outlet for a creative copywriter fascinated by words and their meaning. Here are some real examples of puns in action:

HURRY OVERTURE NEAREST PHONE
[telephone booking service for an orchestra's winter season]

DRAMATIC SAVINGS BARD NONE
[half price ticket offer by the Royal Shakespeare Company]

STICK A TENOR IN SOMEONE'S CARD THIS CHRISTMAS
[advert for theatre gift vouchers]

A BANK FOR PEOPLE WITH VERY LITTLE INTEREST IN BANKS
[advert for a high interest bank account]

GREAT MINDS DRINK ALIKE
[advert for a vitamin drink to boost physical and mental performance]

Jokes and riddles can be a great source of puns.

Q: What's the difference between a jeweller and a jailer?
*A: A jeweller **sells watches** but a jailer **watches cells**. [Groan!]*

Q: What is the difference between a nurse and a tailor?
*A: A nurse **dresses cuts** but a tailor **cuts dresses**.*

Look at puns and analyse how they work. Use them where you can to provide some light relief. But a word of warning: beware unintentional puns.

☒ *NEW! Crash course in driving.*

☒ *We dispense with accuracy*
  [advert for pharmacy]

☒ *Let your children watch as we bake their nan [Indian bread] in front of them*
  [from the family menu at an Indian restaurant]

☒ *There will be a skeleton staff during the cemetery workers' industrial action*

Assonance

Assonance is the repetition of vowel sounds to form an incomplete rhyme. It is subtler than alliteration and only works with vowels in stressed syllables. A famous example is the slogan for the American president Eisenhower (nicknamed 'Ike'):

> *I like Ike.*

A political commentator of the time adapted this to make the point that some people were not sure what policies Eisenhower actually believed in. He came up with this:

> *I like Ike, but what does Ike like?*

Another example from the USA: former President Richard ('Dicky') Nixon was known by some as 'Tricky Dicky'.

Rhyme

Don't overlook old-fashioned rhyme. Remember that rhyme is about *sound*, not spelling. As a result, some adverts using rhyme are better as broadcast ads than on the page.

> *Know of a benefit rip-off? Give us a telephone tip-off. Call the Beat-A-Cheat Line*
> *[an advert for the Government's clampdown on benefits fraud]*
>
> *Deals on Wheels*
> *[headline for customer newsletter article on special offers on cars]*
>
> *Deals on Heels*
> *[ad for discount shoes]*
>
> *Deals on Meals*
> *[advertising special offers at a restaurant]*

Interestingly, 'rhythms' is the longest common word not to have any vowels in it.

Ellipsis

Ellipsis is often used in marketing copy because it's a way of involving your reader in your writing. To produce an ellipsis, omit a word or words that the reader must supply. The missing word(s) must be obvious; otherwise, your copy is meaningless.

> *Hidden inside there's . . . No, that would be telling*
> *[an advert for Rolo truffles]*

The reader deduces that inside the Rolo truffle is a yummy and tasty filling so good it's best kept a secret. Ellipses allow you to say a lot (or to suggest a lot) without using a lot of words. It's more a case of what you don't say. Ellipsis is also the name for the punctuation mark '. . .' (dot dot dot) used in the example above. You don't need to use ellipses in order to produce an elliptical sentence. Take this example:

> ☑ *They don't carry her as far as they used to. But we do*

As lone text, this advert makes no sense. Combined with the London Underground logo and a close-up photo of an elderly woman's legs, supported by a walking stick, we understand the message immediately. It is a short and powerful way of conveying a message and engaging readers by getting them to interpret it.

Here's another example, this time for a restaurant at a smart hotel. The photograph shows a crisp white tablecloth set for dinner and the headline reads:

> *This is starched. Our service isn't.*

Homonyms, heterophones and homophones

Much clever copy is based on the homonym, heterophone or homophone. These are words with the same spelling or pronunciation as another, but a different meaning.

Word	Same Spelling?	Same pronunciation?	Examples
Homophone	☒	☑	Air/heir Bald/bawled Allowed/aloud
Heterophone	☑	☒	Row (propel a boat) Row (argue/quarrel)
Homonym	☑	☑	Row (a line of) Row (propel a boat) Soil (earth) Soil (dirty)

Use these to play on words and create witty copy, especially headlines and slogans. Here's a real life example, a radio advert with a voice-over by actor Vincent Pryce (who often played a vampire in movies):

*You'll love the London Dungeon. I'll **stake** my heart on it.*

This is a good example of a homonym being used as a clever pun: 'stake' meaning both a wager and a sharp wooden stick used for killing vampires.

This car sticker for a Christian organisation works well too:

7 days without prayer makes one weak

And this ad showing a photo of a Scottish lake:

Sainsbury's have discovered that the finest whisky is kept under loch and quay

Antonyms

An antonym is a word that means the opposite of another (a synonym is a word that has the same meaning). Antonyms work well in copy, particularly in adverts and slogans, though they can be used to effect in most copywriting assignments. For example:

*A **little** car with a **big** personality*

***Overspill** your trolley, **underspend** your budget*
[ad for a supermarket]

***High** in taste, **low** in fat*

*A **big** newspaper for a **small** coin*
[used when the Sun reduced its price to 20p]

*Before you **check in**, **check out** our prices*
[ad for duty-free airport shopping]

Use this technique with words that are not quite antonyms:

*Takes **minutes**, lasts **weeks***
[a hair removing cream]

***Half** the size, **twice** the benefit*
[slogan for a new, smaller sized air freshener]

Unexpected deviance

To use this very useful copywriting device, produce a list or series of sentences, each following a pattern. Unexpectedly deviate the last one:

100% customer service
100% quality
100% choice
  0% finance

Top brands
Top service
Top style
Top that!

Here's a witty, real life example from an ad for beer:

Pour homme
Pour femme
Pour down neck

Malapropisms

A malapropism is where a common expression is altered unintentionally, giving it a comic or ludicrous interpretation. (It comes from Mrs Malaprop, a character from Sheridan's play, *The Rivals*.) By changing a word or sound, the original meaning is quite altered. Hilda Ogden in television's *Coronation Street* was famous for her malapropisms, such as calling her mural a 'murial'. Recently a woman noted for putting on airs and graces told me that as her son

tip

You can find some rather rude but hilariously funny spoonerisms by visiting www.fun-with-words.com/spoon erisms_rude.html.

had been awarded an honours degree, she would be going to his granulation ceremony! Other examples include:

- I am on tender hooks.
- It's just a pigment of your imagination.
- She's a wolf in cheap clothing.
- That wench is used lifting heavy loads.

Why not use malapropisms intentionally to produce witty and talked-about adverts? It is a technique that takes some skill, but can work really well.

Spoonerisms

In the same vein as malapropisms are spoonerisms, named after Reverend William Spooner. This academic and cleric was forever getting his words mixed up – slips of the tongue or, if you prefer, tips of the slung. Once, instead of announcing a toast to 'our dear old queen' he proposed: 'Let us drink to the queer old dean'! Spoonerisms can be used to great effect, if you can find an opportunity. Experiment with them if you are at a loss for a creative solution. See what you can come up with. My favourites are 'mean as custard' (keen as mustard), 'bad salad' (sad ballad) and 'flock of bats' (block of flats)!

Common copywriting mistakes and how to avoid them

Every day dreadful copy makes it into print, damaging organisations' reputations and annoying customers. Don't fall foul of the common copywriting blunders. Discover the most frequent mistakes wannabe copywriters make and how to avoid them.

Good copy comes as much from knowing what to avoid as from following what to do! Here are some common errors to look out for:

Over-long text

Long copy is OK, depending on what you are writing. Obviously a book is generally lengthy, whereas a leaflet is not. But what is *too* long? Anything that ends up being longer than it needs to be, due to:

- poor or non-existent editing;
- the inclusion of irrelevant material;
- lack of succinctness;
- sloppy planning.

Over-long copy is unnecessarily time-consuming, taking up too much of your reader's precious time. You run the risk that they will not have the staying power to read all of it. If they give up, you have failed as a copywriter. Make your text as long as it needs to be and no longer. Prune wordy copy. Cut out repetition. Delete superfluous words. Produce a trimmer, leaner version that packs more punch.

Waffle

Call it what you like, waffle or padding dilutes the impact of your message and makes your text longer than it needs to be. The more

> **tip**
>
> Remember that the purpose of writing is to *express*, not to *impress*. Don't get carried away showing off your impressive vocabulary and your knowledge of Latin words and phrases. You'll come across as boastful and alienate your reader.

padding, the less the important sections stand out. Your message gets lost in a mass of cotton wool.

Here's an example of waffle (waffley words in square brackets).

ⓧ *[We would like to point out that] no other company offers [you] the quality and range of products that we do. [You should note that] this offer is only available for a limited [period of] time.*

This example demonstrates how a simple 22-word message gets lost in waffle that adds nothing and brings the word count to a less manageable 36.

Verbosity and officialese

Verbose and bureaucratic words and phrases can creep up on the inexperienced writer, leaving their copy bulging and flabby. For leaner, more succinct text, check your work for verbosity and officialese. Avoid the following:

Flabby	Fit
At this point in time	Now
With regard to/regarding/pertaining to	About
In connection with	About
On a regular basis	Regularly
Please find enclosed	I enclose
Subsequent to	After
Inform	Tell
Terminate	End
Commence	Start/begin
Reside	Live
Endeavour	Try
Assist	Help
Until such time as	Until
Desire	Want
In terms of	Rewrite to avoid, if possible
Relocate	Move
Refreshment facilities	Bar/cafe/restaurant
Parking facilities	Parking
Employment on a part time basis	Part-time work
Prior to	Before
Proceed	Go/walk etc.
Purchase	Buy
Utilise	Use

For the purpose of	For
In order to	To
We would be grateful if	Please
Executive summary	Summary
Owing to the fact that	Because
In the event that	If
In spite of the fact that	Although
In the majority of cases	Usually

The above list is not exhaustive, but you get the idea. Always use short, familiar words rather than longer phrases or 'official' terms – even in official writing. Keep your copy sharp and crisp.

Redundancy/tautology

Redundancy or tautology is where you use superfluous words, needlessly repeating an idea and lengthening your copy. The following are examples of redundancy (the redundant word(s) are in brackets). Avoid them.

- Join (together).
- Meet (up with).
- Divide (up).
- Separate (out).
- Complete the coupon and return (back) to us.
- (Free) gifts.
- Fantastic (new) innovation.
- Don't miss (out on) this fantastic offer.
- Why not try it (out) using our free offer.
- (Advance) planning.
- (Unfilled) vacancy.
- Available in a range of (different) colours.

Redundancy is a sign of sloppy writing and poor editing.

Repetition

Repetition of the same words and phrases indicates slapdash work. It grates on the reader and distracts them from your message. Here's a typical example (with repeated words and phrases underlined):

[x] *We are delighted to announce the _opening_ of another Johnston's Toy Superstore. This year we have _opened_ 20 _stores_ across _Britain_, bringing the total number of _stores_ to 100 in _Britain_. That means there will be a _store near_ you. To _find out_ where your _nearest_ Superstore is, and to _find out_ its _opening_ hours, take a look at the back page of this catalogue where you will _find_ all the information you need.*

There are times when repetition can work to your advantage in marketing copy, reinforcing your message.

☑ *As a very special customer, we'd like to make you a very special offer. We're Britain's best computer dealer, so you'd expect us to offer the best equipment at the best prices.*

☑ *24 hours to play, 24 months to pay*
[car advert offering a day's test drive and two years' interest-free credit]

☑ *NO salesmen. NO commission. NO jargon. NO hassle.*
[advert for a personal equity plan]

Used skilfully and deliberately, repetition can emphasise the point and drive home the message; used by default, it may have the opposite effect.

Clichés

A cliché is an 'off-the-shelf' overused expression or phrase. A master of straight-talking, the late Sir Ernest Gowers wrote in his best selling *The Complete Plain Words*: 'A cliché then is by definition a bad thing, not to be employed by self-respecting writers.' How true! Yet we seem to live by clichés when we speak and when we write. Ban yourself from using them and see how you struggle! The cliché is a lazy solution. Be imaginative. Don't dredge up common and overused phrases: invent your own. Make your copy fresh and readable, not stale and hackneyed.

Here's an example of the type of thing you should avoid, albeit a rather exaggerated one:

☒ *We might all be enjoying this Indian summer, with winter thoughts far from our mind. But the colder months are just round the corner. Keep warm as toast this winter with a 'living flame' gas fire. During the next cold snap, your neighbours will be green with envy when they see how cosy your lounge is compared with their own. So if you want to be snug as a bug in a rug when Jack Frost calls, get your living flame brochure now.*

You can turn clichés on their head, transforming them into witty ditties. Take this example:

☑ *The Bucks Start Here*
[advert for an investment product]

Marketing clichés

Some publicity material is littered with marketing clichés, occasionally being little more than a string of clichés linked by the odd conjunction. For writing that is fresh and vital, avoid them. They add nothing. Body-swerve these common marketing clichés:

- The best that money can buy
- An opportunity not to be missed
- Never to be repeated
- Chance/offer of a lifetime
- A new concept in . . .
- A warm welcome awaits you at . . .
- A dream holiday/kitchen
- A unique opportunity
- We are delighted to announce
- It is our pleasure to offer you
- A truly amazing
- As a valued customer.

Very

Using the word 'very' can be a weak way of expressing yourself. The more you use it, the weaker it becomes. Usually there are better ways of expressing intensity than tacking 'very' before an adjective. 'Very hot' is better described as: baking; sweltering; scorching; sizzling . . . 'Very tired' is weaker than: exhausted; fatigued; worn out; done-in; weary; blitzed; zonked.

Ambiguity

For copy to communicate, what *you* write must be what *they* read: the message the reader receives must be the same as the one you transmitted. Never assume that the two will coincide: they frequently do not. Even professionally-written copy sometimes contains ambiguity – where the chosen words have two or more meanings or interpretations, or the meaning is unclear.

[X] *For an annual subscription of just £20 you can get Gardening Times delivered direct to your door, bi-monthly.*

Does this mean that you get a magazine every two months (six issues in a year), or twice every month (24 annually)? It makes a big difference!

Here's another example:

☒ *Introducing two great new products:*

- *our precision tile cutter and*
- *our one-step grout*

Both cost just £20 . . .

£20 each? £20 for the two? Ambiguous wording loses sales. People will not have the time or inclination to write or phone to check the details, so they won't order. Or they might equate sloppy writing with a sloppy product. Either way, you lose.

Skilful writers deliberately use ambiguity to create clever and memorable copy, as in this example from a TV advert:

A woman offers the conceited man coffee during a business meeting. He asks if she has any decaffeinated. She makes the coffee and the man tastes his.

Man: I see you didn't have decaffeinated then!
Woman: No, but you did.

At first, the viewer thinks the man has been given non-decaffeinated coffee. When the woman speaks, we realise that the coffee he had was in fact decaffeinated. This is a neat way of saying: 'Our decaffeinated coffee is so good it has all the taste of non-decaffeinated coffee.' Deliberate ambiguity in this context is a powerful tool; in any other, it is a grave mistake.

Hype

Much marketing material is little more than hype, containing exaggerated, misleading, or even false claims. It can be tempting to overplay the benefits of a product or service, particularly if it is actually rather dull. Hyping enables a copywriter to turn a dreary assignment into one with a bit more zip. But resist overselling. It

TRUE STORY

On a Turkish holiday, I saw an exotic-sounding item on a restaurant menu. The waiter explained that it was a delicious dessert made with the finest fresh produce: eggs, cane sugar, milk, flour and one or two other ingredients. Seduced, I ordered one. What arrived was a dried-up square of sponge cake! The goods failed to live up to the description. I forgave the waiter, who was, after all, communicating in English, a foreign language to him. But what's your excuse?

leads to disappointment when your readers inevitably discover that your claims were nothing more than embellishment. Disappointment creates unhappy customers, and unhappy customers eventually lead to an organisation's downfall.

Here are two real-life examples of hype:

A traditional unleavened bread lightly stroked with olive oil, smothered with a delicious paste made from fresh Italian tomatoes, topped with succulent buffalo cheese and sprinkled with sundried rosemary and basil, then baked in special ovens.
[a frozen pizza packaging]

[flyer for a craft and DIY magazine]
[picture of ordinary flower display] Make a bewitching topiary
[photo of two wooden shelves] Conjure up a set of attractive and stylish shelves that will amaze and impress

Pomposity

Perfectly nice people can take on a self-important air when they pick up a pen and begin to write. These otherwise down-to-earth people come across as pompous asses, with their highfalutin language or obsequious phrases. This stems from an erroneous belief that the written word should be formal and grand-sounding. There's little place for this kind of writing in any situation, and no room for it in copywriting. It sounds ridiculous! The following example, though fictitious, is all too typical of what is produced:

HERMITAGE RESTAURANT
The discerning client will appreciate the effort the Hermitage team has put into making the dining experience at our restaurant truly unrivalled and unforgettable. Maitre d' prides himself on the crisp, starched tablecloths upon which our guests are served, silver service of course, a delectable luncheon. Connoisseurs will delight at the Hermitage's finest and extensive wine list. Those with a sweet tooth will be overjoyed at the choice of superlative desserts on offer.

Take care and these common copywriting mistakes are easily avoided. Here are some other things you should steer clear of when you write.

No offence intended

Copy that offends will not sell. Usually any offence caused is unintentional, so be vigilant and if in doubt, err on the side of caution. The

TRUE STORY

A crane hire company wanted an advert for the trade press to encourage contractors to avoid potentially dangerous equipment by hiring from a reputable firm like them. Their ad showed a smiling girl next to an open car door, with the headline: 'Don't take lifts from strangers!'. Following a complaint, the ASA considered the advert and deemed it unsuitable, given fears and concern about child abduction.

ASA (Advertising Standards Authority) commissions research into what causes offence. Its latest findings, of non-broadcast advertising, show that nearly 20% of people have been personally offended by non-broadcast advertising they have seen in the last 12 months, and nearly a third have seen ads that they believe would offend others. In total, four-fifths of respondents believed that advertising sometimes goes too far and offends.

Here's what to watch out for if you want to avoid offence:

Four-letter words

Bad language is a no-no, even if used humorously. Attitude research carried out by the ASA showed that even relatively mild swear words like pillock, git, bloody and damn were found to be unacceptable in posters and other advertising. Even those who swear can find expletives offensive in other people's writing.

TRUE STORY

A complaint against an ad for Virgin cola was upheld, even though the offending word was not in English. The ad appeared on the day of a big football match (England vs. Spain), in a tabloid's sports pages. It read: 'Eres una mierda aaaaargh! Trans: What a fine Spanish team you are!' Of course, its real meaning is a little coarser (consult your Spanish dictionary!). So tread carefully and be sensitive.

No sex please, we're British

You've heard the expression 'sex sells'. When writing copy, be reminded that sex also offends. Independent research on behalf of the Advertising Standards Authority found that over 75% of respondents believed that it was wrong to use sex to sell unconnected products.

Never use sex as an attention-grabber, as in this real life example:

[photograph of young woman leaning against piano wearing a short dress, which had ridden up to expose part of her bare buttocks. Captioned:]

GENTLEMEN NOW WE HAVE YOUR ATTENTION, WE WOULD LIKE TO ANNOUNCE THE ARRIVAL OF THE NEW SEASON COLLECTIONS . . .

Sex used in this way amounts to poor copy on two counts. First, it causes offence and thus loses you custom. Secondly, the picture might attract attention, but does the advert arouse interest in the product, desire to own the product, and action to buy the product? No. Sex might attract attention, but cannot achieve a sale. An image of any sort may grab the eye, but it's good copy that keeps it there.

TRUE STORY

There are always some people who see sexual innuendo where none exists. When Durex ran an advert for condoms on the London Underground, it provoked some bizarre complaints. The ad showed an embracing couple and a 'thought bubble'. One person complained that the thought bubble seemed to represent discharged semen! Another said that the person sitting below the ad would be seen to be thinking about sex! You can't please them all!

Kiss of death

Death is a no-go area (unless you are promoting an undertaker's service!). An advert for a song called 'Roll Over and Die' showed a large kitchen knife beside the song lyrics, which included 'If you can't take this there's only one way out . . .' and continued in this vein. Complaints to the ASA resulted.

In another case (which also prompted complaints to the ASA), an advert offered West End offices rent-free. A photo of a man holding a pistol to his head was captioned: 'Imagine the consequences if you miss this opportunity.'

Pork pies

Misleading or downright dishonest ads will land you and your organisation in trouble. A hotel claimed to be 'Torquay's highest rated seafront 3 star hotel', despite there being another equally rated seafront hotel nearby. Misleading copy will lose you custom – guaranteed.

Unfunny humour

Humour is a subjective matter. I have a rather juvenile sense of humour, but I am aware that not everyone shares it. When writing for others, be mindful of sensitivities. What's funny to you may be distressing to others. I was amused by an advert for a soft drink that showed a woman leaning over a man and kissing him. The headline read: 'If I suck hard enough I might get my Irn-Bru back.' It made me laugh, but it made 46 people angry enough to complain to the ASA.

Humour's a fantastic creative device, and some of our most successful ads have been based on it, but effective use requires talent. Even the professionals sometimes get it wrong. Take the ad written for IBM by a leading ad agency. It claimed that a computer's speakers were a 'thundering 30-watt', 'wall-shaking' and that they were 'one way to meet the neighbours'. This approach was not shared by the person who reported them to the ASA, or by the ASA itself, who considered that the ad condoned noise pollution.

Courting controversy

Some organisations thrive on controversy, but it's a risky approach. Controversy is generally best avoided, though that doesn't mean you have to be bland. Sometimes there is a place for a shocking or thought-provoking approach. Independent research for the ASA shows that most people (87%) appear to be more tolerant of thought-provoking shock tactics and distressing images when used by charities and government to promote a good cause, while they are very much against shocking messages in commercial advertising.

TRUE STORY

An advert for an internet access provider pictured a pill above the headline: 'We supply speed to techno-junkies'. The reference to illegal drugs was considered inappropriate and the advertisers were asked by the ASA to amend their advert.

---

tip

Take a look at the ASA's website for examples of offending ads and advice on how to avoid causing offence (www.asa.org.uk).

Religion

If people wish to remain friends, they are advised to avoid discussing religion and politics. Religious allusion in copy can land you in trouble. People take religion very seriously and don't like it being used in anything as trivial and consumerist as marketing material. Copy that in any way uses religious allusion is strongly objected to by some members of the public. Don't risk offending. Avoid religion (unless you are promoting a church or mosque!)

Becoming a copy critic

To excel in copywriting it helps to be interested in the subject. You must understand what works, what fails, what stands out as top-notch copy and why. In short, you need finely tuned critical skills, both to assess your own work and to learn from others. This chapter will help you develop these skills.

Do you often look at a piece of marketing material and think: 'Wow! That's brilliant. Wish I'd written that!'? Yes? Good. No? Time you started! Professional copywriters are 'copy-aware'. Make sure you're constantly on the lookout for other people's copy, ever eager to dissect it, to analyse it, to understand it, to be critical of it, to learn from it. Never let marketing copy wash over you. Don't idly eye adverts or scan direct mailshots. Stop looking at copy as a punter and start applying your professional analytical skills. Regard yourself as a copy scientist. Identify the techniques used. Understand what makes a particular piece of writing great and what makes another one mediocre.

Once you reach the state of being 'copy-aware', you will see a vast improvement in your own work for remarkably little effort. Copywriting will become more instinctive. This will subconsciously influence and improve your own work. You will find yourself in an upward spiral, writing ever better copy and gaining in confidence as your ability grows.

Seven simple steps to copy awareness

1. Assemble piles of newspapers and magazines. Cut out the ads from them.
2. Place effective ads in one pile and poor ads in another.

3. Repeat the process using brochures, direct mail and other marketing material.
4. Nip out with a digital camera and photograph a selection of good and bad billboard ads, adverts on buses and in shop windows.
5. Analyse the good materials. Try to understand why they are good. Has the copywriter used particular techniques that are well suited to the medium? Have they approached the task from a novel or innovative angle? Do words and pictures work in harmony?
6. Repeat the process with the poor publicity material. What makes something inferior? Is it too long? Wrong language? Wrong message? Be specific.
7. Have a go at rewriting the bad examples if you have time. What techniques can you use to spice up flat copy or to make weak material hard-hitting?

Have a go yourself

I have put together a mix of real and made-up examples of good and bad copy. The made-up examples are based on real copy and are similar to the sort of marketing material being turned out by many organisations. Read through them. For the examples of bad copy, write down:

■ What is wrong with each one (be as detailed as possible).
■ Whether there is anything good/any redeeming features (specify them).

(When you have worked through the examples, look at the end of the chapter to compare your notes.)

The bad

Example 1

This comprises real extracts from a publicity brochure for a down-at-heel London hotel. (I have changed the name to protect the guilty!)

Dear guest,

On behalf of the Management and Staff, may I take this opportunity to welcome you to the Boswall Park Hotel . . .

We want to make your visit to the Boswall Park Hotel a memorable occasion, and it is our desire that every guest should receive entire satisfaction during their stay. Our caring and friendly staff will attend to your every comfort, always with the personalised style that will endear you to our hotel.

This Guest Directory of Hotel Services in your bedroom describes all other facilities available in the Hotel. This elegant international hotel offers the discerning traveller the attention to detail and standards of service they would expect. Bedrooms have been beautifully designed and furnished to the highest standard of luxury. All bedrooms feature the modern-day facilities expected of a luxury hotel, including a hair dryer and trouser press. The Tulip Bar has a superb collection of beverages and is the perfect venue for a relaxation . . .

Our aim is to provide the highest standards of service and hospitality, with the comfort and facilities you would expect of modern luxury hotels, while preserving the traditional character of the properties themselves. If you wish to have any further information please do not hesitate to contact myself or any member of my staff. I take this opportunity to wish you a very enjoyable stay at the Boswall Park Hotel.

Example 2

This is a (fictitious) newspaper advert for a new magazine.

OPTIONS: GET IT!

Options is the newest magazine to hit newsagents. Majoring on information every home-owner will want, from new wallpaper to getting a better deal on your mortgage, Options will have all the answers . . . and more! Free gift with first issue. Buy it today!

Example 3

This is a fictitious direct mail letter:

Dear Mrs Smith,

Here is an opportunity not to be missed. We are offering you the chance of a lifetime – a dream cruise on the Nile. Yes, this fantastic trip is the first prize in an exclusive competition being offered to anyone ordering from the enclosed catalogue before the end of December.

Imagine it. Relaxing on a sun lounger on the deck of a five-star luxury cruise boat as you glide past historic temples. Visit the treasures of Tutankhamun, the temple of Philae, the Colossi of Memnon. Haggle in the souks and bazaars. Marvel at the splendours of the ancient world. All this can be yours if your entry is lucky enough to be picked. Anyone ordering from the catalogue will automatically be entered in the draw.

> You will see from the catalogue that we offer an unrivalled range of travel goods. Everything from mosquito repellent to travel plugs. From suitcases to passport holders. Every item you could possibly need for holidays at home and abroad can be found in our catalogue. So place your order now!
>
> Yours sincerely
>
> *Thomas Tobias*
>
> Thomas Tobias
> **Promotions Manager**

The good

Sometimes it can be a confidence boost to see just how badly other people write! You realise that your skills are better than you thought. But now for a look at some good copy, again featuring a mix of real and made-up examples. Work out what makes the copy effective. Compare notes with me at the end of the chapter.

Example 1

The headline from an advert for a development of luxury flats, which showed someone in front of the flats playing a saxophone:

Makes Other Penthouses Sound A Little Flat!

Example 2

Slogan from advert for an upright vacuum cleaner:

The Upright that's Downright Good

Example 3

Extract from an article in a customer newsletter. Produced by a fictitious company running theme parks and leisure complexes:

Keep your kids entertained

Six quick, easy and cheap ways to avoid boredom this summer

School holidays can be great fun . . . until the boredom sets in. Day after day of the kids under your feet, getting into mischief, running out of things to keep them occupied. Despair not! Make this summer different. Give your children a time to remember, without breaking the bank.

Here are half a dozen ways of keeping your under-12s entertained.

1. Craftwork

Kids love craftwork. Save up all your old card, ribbon, washing up liquid bottles, cereal boxes, loo roll tubes etc. Buy a huge tub of glue, a ball of string and a selection of poster paints. They'll make an almighty mess, but it will keep your kids quiet and entertained for hours – and you'll be nurturing their creative side!

Cost: £7.50 for enough materials to keep four children busy for days

2. Tommy's theme park

Escape the real world and enter the realms of fantasy at Tommy's Theme Park. Experience weightlessness on our moon walk. Swim with crocodiles in our swamp simulator. Chat with a dinosaur in our primeval forest. Adults and children will love every minute of it. Guaranteed!

Cost: £25 for two adults and two children.

3. Nature trail

Draw up a list of items and pack your kids off to the back garden or a local park on a nature trail to find them. You might include: toadstools; buttercups; daisies; ivy; moss; ants; spiders; beetles. Have a prize for the child who finds all the items first. Have runner-up prizes for everyone else to prevent punch-ups afterwards!

Cost: Free!

Comparing notes

The bad

Example 1: hotel brochure

This example is dreadful, yet it is all too typical of marketing material written in-house. It breaks all the rules of good copy and has no redeeming features.

- **Too wordy** – Why write: 'On behalf of the Management and Staff, may I take this opportunity to welcome you to the Boswall Park Hotel . . . 'when a simple 'Welcome to the Boswall Park Hotel' is sufficient?
- **Too stuffy** – Stuffy expressions like 'on behalf of' and 'may I take this opportunity' make no impact.
- **Too pompous** – Grandiose statements such as 'it is our desire' sound insincere.
- **Stating the obvious** – 'This Guest Directory of Hotel Services in your bedroom . . .' You are in your bedroom reading a directory entitled Directory of Hotel Services. You don't need to be told that! Nor that the bar sells 'beverages'.
- **Incorrect initial capitalisation** – Words like 'Staff' and 'Hotel Services' do not need capital letters unless they are at the beginning of a sentence.
- **Obsequiousness** – Fawning phrases such as 'the discerning traveller' sound absurd in a down-at-heel hotel.
- **Ridiculous claims** – Hairdryers and trouser presses are hardly the height of luxury!
- **Long, unflowing sentences** – See in particular the sentence: 'Our aim is to provide the highest standards of service and hospitality, with the comfort and facilities you would expert of modern luxury hotels, while preserving the traditional character of the properties themselves.'
- **Hype** – Claiming that a shabby hotel in Earl's Court is a luxury, elegant international hotel is tommyrot. Writing nice things doesn't make them true!

Example 2: advert for new magazine

On the plus side, this advert is not too wordy. But that's probably its only redeeming feature!

- **Headline** – This fails to do its job. It does not flag up or attract the attention of the intended audience: people who are interested in their homes.
- **Incomplete** – The advert mentions a free gift, but not what it is. Frequency of publication is omitted.
- **Tense** – Use of the present tense would give the copy a much-needed lift.
- **Call to action** – 'Buy it today!' is a weak call to action. Say where it can be bought and how much it will cost.

Here's the ad again, and underneath it is a better alternative:

OPTIONS: GET IT!

Options is the newest magazine to hit newsagents. Majoring on information every home-owner will want, from new wallpaper to getting a better deal on your mortgage, Options will have all the answers . . . and more! Free gift with first issue. Buy it today!

HOMEOWNERS: NEW MAGAZINE AND FREE GIFT

Want to save money on your mortgage? Like to know about best buys in home furnishings? Then Options is for you! Packed full of tips and advice on every aspect of owning a home, from the financial side through to interior design, it is available monthly at all branches of WH Smith and John Menzies. Issue 1 is on sale now with free 'star' stencil. Only £2. Don't miss it!

Example 3: direct mail letter promoting travel catalogue

Is this a mailing for a travel goods catalogue? You could be forgiven for thinking that it's promoting an Egyptian cruise! Were I to rewrite the letter, I would produce something more along the following lines:

Dear Mrs Smith,

LIKE TRAVELLING? THEN YOU'LL LOVE THIS CATALOGUE

It might even win you a trip to Egypt!

If you like to travel – at home or abroad – you'll love our new catalogue (enclosed). Everything even the most seasoned traveller could possibly want is in it – from tummy pills to travel plugs, and mosquito nets to medical insurance, it's all here. What's more, if you place an order before the end of December, we'll automatically enter you in our prize draw to win a family Nile cruise.

Imagine it. Relaxing on a sun lounger on the deck of a five-star luxury cruise boat as you glide past historic temples. Visit the treasures of Tutankhamun, the temple of Philae, the Colossi of Memnon. Haggle in the souks and bazaars. Marvel at the splendours of the ancient world. Place an order and your family could enjoy all this.

Take a look through the catalogue. We're sure you will be delighted with our unrivalled range and affordable prices. And remember, you might get more than you bargained for if your name is picked out of the hat!

Yours sincerely

Thomas Tobias

Thomas Tobias
Promotions Manager

PS Remember to place your order by the end of December if you want to enter our exclusive draw for a family trip to Egypt.

- **Wrong focus** – The original version focused too much on the prize draw, mentioning the product (the catalogue) almost incidentally.
- **Missed tricks** – It failed to use direct mail techniques, such as the headline and hand-written style postscript to flag up and reinforce the message.
- **Clichéd** – The first part of the letter was filled with marketing clichés. In its favour, the middle paragraph was not too bad – but no one will read as far as a middle paragraph unless the preceding paragraphs have gripped them.

The good

Example 1: advert for penthouse flats

A few simple words combine to form an attention-grabbing headline that succinctly conveys some key messages.

- **Clever** – A neat little pun on the words 'little flat'.
- **Succinct** – A few words get across the point.
- **Key messages** – A short headline obliquely conveys two key messages (1. penthouses for sale – the word 'penthouse' conjures up images of luxury – and 2. other properties are inferior).

Example 2: vacuum cleaner slogan

This is everything a slogan should be:

- **Clever** – Slogans must be memorable and this one is, thanks to its clever play on words: upright/downright
- **Key messages** – It conveys the message that it is an upright cleaner and that it is a very good cleaner.
- **Succinct** – Key information is communicated in a lively way using a few words.

Example 3: newsletter article

Too many customer newsletters bore their readers with glowing prose about the company. This article starts from the reader's perspective. Instead of telling them how great the theme parks and leisure complexes are, it starts with a useful article full of ways of keeping children entertained during the long summer holiday. As part of the article, the company quite reasonably promotes its wares, but it does not ram them down the reader's throat. They are merely presented as options. This soft sell approach works well in customer newsletters.

Now that you have honed your critical skills, apply them to your own work. Gather copy you have produced in the past. Analyse and dissect it. Spot your weak points. See how you can improve it.

Finding the creative you

Do you have a creative writer inside you struggling to get out? Find out in this chapter how to unlock the creative you. Discover where to look for inspiration. Have a go with different writing styles, using a series of exercises designed to develop your creativity.

Children are amazingly creative. They draw and paint, build models, play act, even make up new words. Sadly this innate creativity disappears with age. We become self-conscious and inhibited so that by the time we reach adulthood many of us have forgotten how to be creative. Thankfully creativity can be restored!

Sometimes creativity comes from within. A brilliant idea emerges unprompted. At other times, a catalyst is required to spark an idea or to create the right mood.

tip

Examine how professional copywriters approach an assignment. Look at marketing material and see if you can work out how the copywriter arrived at the finished item. Try to map out the process involved. See if you can apply those steps when you have a new assignment.

Inspiration and ideas

I have an 'inspiration box' which acts as my catalyst. It's just a cardboard box, but it's filled with material that has inspired me – press ads, leaflets, annual reports, posters, cards, direct mail packages . . . anything at all that I have been impressed with. On days when I am not feeling very inspired, I reach for my cardboard box and delve in. Soon my mind is buzzing with ideas. Remember that the idea of an inspiration box is to prompt, not plagiarise.

I also have an ideas box. This shoebox contains my own ideas. Whenever I have an idea, however crazy, I write it down on a small piece of paper and put it in the shoebox. When I'm in need of a good idea, I tip the contents of the box on my desk and see what's there. Sometimes I can lift an idea, or I may have to adapt it. I frequently find that the ideas act as catalysts for new, unrelated ideas.

Word games

Some copywriters play word games to warm themselves up and get their creative juices flowing. They might invent collective nouns or amusing spoonerisms.

Subway prophets

In 'The Sound of Silence' Paul Simon wrote: 'the words of the prophets are written on the subway walls'. Some of the best lines I have read appeared not in slick advertising, but on the walls of public lavatories. Putting aside the less salubrious offerings, there are some real gems – 'If God hadn't intended us to write on walls, he would have never given us the example' and 'in the beginning was the word. And the word was Aardvark'. It seems to me that if people can write readable copy on the lavvy, then anyone can be a copywriter! But seriously, graffiti can be creative, particularly the way it grows as people add to it.

Getting your surroundings right

Environment is important for a copywriter. Great copy rarely comes from a noisy and busy, open plan, strip-lit office. Soft lighting, peace and no interruptions to interrupt the flow – that's the kind of environment likely to produce words with fizz. Writing is as much an art as a craft, and writers need the right environment to stimulate their creativity. Try to create a workspace that will nurture your creativity, not strangle it.

Creativity-boosting exercises

Work through these exercises in any order you like. Don't be put off by any that prove difficult. It's only by taxing yourself that you will improve your writing skills. Place each completed exercise in a

> **tip**
>
> Some people force themselves to come up with a thought or idea each day. The crazier and less inhibited, the better. These thoughts, ideas and observations are pinned up around their office, and colleagues and visitors are invited to add to or develop them.

> **tip**
>
> Expand your vocabulary. Learn a new word every day.

TRUE STORY

French novelist Balzac would not write unless he had an unripe apple on his desk! Many writers have their foibles. They may be famous authors, while you are just a humble wannabe copywriter. But what the heck! Indulge yourself if it helps. But don't take it too far. You can succumb a little to artistic temperament, but always maintain a businesslike discipline that ensures you get the job done.

ringbinder. Whenever you feel your confidence waning, pull out your ringbinder and remind yourself of the wide range of writing assignments you have tackled.

Exercise 1 – children's story

Assignment

Write a 12-page children's storybook that will appeal to the average four-year-old. Use language appropriate for the age group. Do not exceed 600 words. The final book will be illustrated. Indicate clearly what text and what illustrations will be on each page. Ensure each illustration complements the words.

What you will learn

- How to use a different writing style.
- How to write for a well defined audience with very particular needs.
- How to use appropriate language.
- How to ensure words and pictures work in harmony (see next chapter for more information on this).
- How to communicate a lot of information in a lively manner using just a few words.

Exercise 2 – adjectives

Assignment

Think of 15 suitable, appealing adjectives to describe each of the following products:

- expensive perfume
- cheap baked beans
- an exclusive brand of caviar
- an affordable 'run-around' hatchback car
- a top of the range Jaguar car
- a girl's doll
- a boy's doll such as Action Man
- an office swivel chair
- a brand new machine for making nuts and bolts
- an MP3 player.

What you will learn

If you are having difficulty writing a piece of copy, it can sometimes help to start by listing suitable adjectives, as a warm-up to get you in the right frame of mind. It can also spark an idea, which you can develop when you come to writing your copy. This exercise should tax your word power to the limit.

Exercise 3 – synonyms

Assignment

Complete the following exercise without a thesaurus. Think of as many synonyms as possible for each of the following words:

- children
- box
- money
- exhibition
- seat
- happy
- empty
- end.

What you will learn

Amateur copywriters frequently repeat the same words instead of finding alternatives in order to avoid monotonous text. The challenge for copywriters is to come up with different ways of saying the same thing, and that's where synonyms come in. Become skilled at using synonyms and always have a thesaurus at your side when you work. (Most word-processing programs incorporate a thesaurus, but the paper version will probably be more comprehensive, or a decent one on CD.) When you are writing and there is a risk of repetition, list the words you will need to repeat and come up with alternatives. Select from your list of alternatives when you start to write.

Exercise 4 – crossword clues

Assignment

Here is a completed crossword. Come up with cryptic clues for each of the answers.

Across

1

3

6

8

Down

1

2

4

5

7

What you will learn

By having to provide definitions to everyday words, you will learn how to be precise and clear with language. You will also learn how to play with words.

Exercise 5 – period-style copy

Assignment

Have you ever looked through old newspapers and magazines and smiled at the outmoded adverts? Even ads from the '60s and '70s look outdated, let alone those from the 1900s or 1920s.

Imagine you are working on a press advert for washing powder. Step into a time machine and speed back to the 1920s. Write an ad in an appropriate style for the period. Then do one for the same washing powder, but this time in a 1960s' style. Finally, write the sort of ad that might be used today. Write the copy and indicate where visuals/graphics will go and what they will show.

What you will learn

Sometimes advertisers use a 'period'-style advert. Because it looks or sounds so different, it stands out from the contemporary and attracts attention. Attention is all-important if you want your copy noticed. Use a period feel for newsletters and annual reports, especially where you are celebrating an important anniversary such as 25 years or a centenary. A customer newsletter produced with sepia tinted photos, genuine company ads from the 1890s, and text written in a Victorian style could be a great and memorable gimmick. A fab and groovy psychedelic annual report to celebrate the anniversary of an organisation founded in the Swinging Sixties would have the same effect.

Exercise 6 – rhyme and alliteration

Assignment: part 1

You are working for a dog food manufacturer called Bonzo. Write a short press ad for the product that features rhyme.

Assignment: part 2

Now write a slogan for the same dog food, this time using alliteration.

What you will learn

Rhyme can be used to good effect in marketing copy. Remember the 'Lipsmackin' thirstquenchin' . . .' Pepsi advert from the '70s? I remember people trying to learn the words, and others wearing T-shirts with the rhyme printed across. It can be difficult to use rhyme well, so practise as much as you can.

Slogans are powerful and slogan-writing is an art. Key components are that they must be memorable, meaningful, original, positive, believable, snappy and apt.

tip

To see a massive collection of slogans, consult *Slogans* (edited by Laurence Urdang and Celia Dame Robbins, Gale Research Company, 1984.) This collection of over 6,000 slogans used in advertising, political campaigns and so on is arranged by thematic categories such as aerospace, shampoo, coffee and furniture. To analyse the effectiveness of your own slogans, visit www.adslogans.com/slogananalysis and use the free, online diagnostic tool.

Exercise 7 – product names

Assignment: part 1

Come up with three suitable product names for each of the following:

- A range of luxury cat food with recipes devised by a leading, upmarket chef.
- A new over-the-counter drug to eliminate flatulence.
- A lightweight and affordable mobile crane for use on small building sites.

Assignment: part 2

Here are two products:

- A nippy little hatchback car that's perfect for city driving.
- A luxury executive car with leather seats and walnut dashboard.

Here are two product names:

- the Churchill
- the Zipper.

Assign each of the products with the appropriate product name. Write an explanation of why you chose which name for which product.

What you will learn

Some companies spend thousands, tens or even hundreds of thousands on developing the right product names. Some words have strong connotations and are chosen for this reason. This exercise gets you to think about the hidden meaning of words and how a simple word can conjure up so much more, adding subtle meaning to a product.

TRUE STORY

When did you last see a Vauxhall Nova? Probably quite a few years ago. The car manufacturer had to abandon this name and change it to Corsa because Nova meant 'no go' in Spanish!

Exercise 8 – limericks

Assignment

I read my first limerick, aged six, in my Basil Brush annual. It went something like this:

> There was a young woman from Twickenham
> Whose shoes were too tight to walk quick in 'em
> Once, after a walk
> Looking whiter than chalk
> She took 'em both off and got sick in 'em

Write an amusing limerick about a copywriter.

What you will learn

Copywriters need to be able to turn their hand to anything. Most of your work will be straight prose, but there may be times when you have to adopt a gimmicky style. This exercise will show you that you can do the silliest assignment with aplomb!

Exercise 9 – collective nouns

Assignment

I heard a radio programme in which listeners were asked to come up with a collective noun for the smokers who huddle outside their smoke-free offices for a sly ciggie. My two favourites were cigeratti and fagarazzi. Come up with two of your own.

What you will learn

This exercise will get you to think about language in a creative way. Sometimes marketing copy requires words to be invented and this exercise will give you experience of the technique.

Exercise 10 – made-up words

Assignment

This assignment builds upon the previous one. Toddlers are brilliant at inventing funny, nonsense words that are cunningly apt and their meaning immediately clear. When my son was small, he would 'schoosh' me with his water pistol. What a wonderfully onomatopoeic word! Growing up in Edinburgh, he was familiar with the bum-crunching sensation of crossing cobblestone streets in his pushchair. When descending the stairs on his backside (as most two-year-olds do!), he'd describe it as 'cobbling'. This precocious linguistic creativity is lost when we become self-conscious adults. Revive it by making up some words of your own. Devise at least five new words, along with definitions.

What you will learn

Sometimes memorable copy uses made-up words. Adverts for Smint mints use the made-up word 'sminted' as a verb in their slogan 'Have you been sminted?' You might find that a made-up word can help your organisation get noticed.

TRUE STORY

The manufacturer of Whiskas cat food coined the word 'catisfaction' to describe the effect their delicious food produces in felines. Apt made-up words are a good way to get your copy noticed. Traditional china-maker Wedgwood was promoting an avant-garde teapot in an ad. A photo of the teapot, with the word 'Wedgwouldn't?' said it all.

Exercise 11 – evocative writing

Assignment: part 1

You have just opened a portion of delicious chip shop chips, wrapped in paper, and generously sprinkled with salt and vinegar. Describe how they:

- look: their appearance, colour, texture
- smell
- taste
- feel on your fingers.

Be as descriptive and evocative as you can.

Assignment: part 2

Repeat the exercise, but substitute the chips with one of your organisation's products. Ignore any of the senses that do not apply, and add sound to the list, if appropriate.

What you will learn

Your powers of description lie at the heart of your ability to write copy that communicates with readers. This is particularly important where you are selling an experience, though it could be argued that the senses come into play for all products and many services.

Here's how you can use the power of the senses to write copy that has more punch.

☑ *A deserted golden tropical beach bathed in silver moonlight. Blue sea lapping gently over pink coral. Warm breezes wafting fragrant scents of jasmine and ylang ylang flowers. This is Bariba, the most beautiful Caribbean island.*

This passage involves the reader. It takes them to the island and lets them experience the sights, sounds and smells. Compare it with this:

☒ *Bariba Island is a Caribbean island that offers peace and tranquillity for those seeking a holiday away from the cut and thrust of city life.*

Something's lacking in this version: sensation. Always show, don't just tell.

Exercise 12 – clichés

Assignment

Rewrite the following clichés in your own words.

What you will learn

Clichés are a lazy writer's solution. Wordsmiths who can't be bothered to be original grab a ready-assembled string of words off the shelf and use those instead. Whenever you reach for a cliché, stop. Tailor-made is always better. Rewrite the cliché so that you express the sentiment but using fresh words that will make your reader sit up and take notice.

- Sick as a parrot.
- Don't put off to tomorrow what you can do today.
- There's no place like home.
- Love is blind.
- Up the creek without a paddle.

From these exercises, you will gain experience of a wide range of copywriting assignments that will help you increase your word-smithing skills. Put your work to one side, then repeat the exercises again in a month's time. Compare the two and see how you've progressed.

CHAPTER 10

Words and design in harmony

Whether it is a press advert or a sales brochure, most of what you write will be professionally designed. This chapter will explain how to work with graphic designers to produce text that is harmonious with design. Pick up tips on how to write the sort of copy that not only reads well, but also looks good on the printed page.

Choosing and using the right words is what copywriting is all about. But effective publicity material requires more than well-chosen words. Most marketing material is a combination of words blended with photos, illustrations and other designed images. Great words lost in lousy layout = inferior and ineffective marketing material. Ensure your words work at full capacity by teaming them up with first-rate design.

Design must:

- make the most of the words;
- add something extra to the words, so that they become more than the sum of their parts;
- enhance text through sympathetic and harmonious design.

Copy and design are equal but different partners. Text that ignores design, or design that ignores text, is doomed. The copywriter must be design-aware. Understand the part design can play in marketing material. Keep in mind the devices you can use to get copy and design working well together. Have design firmly in your mind as you write your copy. Copywriters working in partnership with designers produce the best marketing material. Write copy without regard to design and you cannot expect a harmonious result. Powerful publicity will elude you.

> **tip**
>
> A decent space between lines – this is called 'leading' – increases readability by 12%. Tell your designer!

Writing with an eye to design is not difficult: you don't have to be both designer and wordsmith. Simply try to think in words *and* pictures. As you write, bear in mind how design can:

- Give the necessary prominence and impact to key words, sentences or paragraphs on the page.
- Give the correct emphasis to each part of your writing.
- Draw attention to the most important sections.
- Create a visual eye-path so your reader is led through the copy in the right order.
- Make your text easy to read and easy on the eye.
- Provide meaning or emotion more powerfully than words alone.

Sometimes it's impossible to write copy until you have an image of the finished design in your head. Take the following examples. In the first, an ad for a motoring device to warn of traffic jams within a 10-mile radius, the headline reads:

Rapid Relief from the Misery of Congestion

The photo (the main focus of the ad) shows cars bumper-to-bumper in a mega traffic snarl-up. The headline on its own could refer to a flu remedy; the accompanying photograph gives a comic new meaning. Without the mental picture of a traffic jam, the copywriter would not have devised this witty headline. Here's another example:

Avoid painful fillings

This ad shows a car alongside a petrol pump. The body copy explains how fuel-efficient the car is. The copywriter had design in mind when creating this line. Think visually as well as verbally and the doors to creativity will open. Give yourself the opportunity to let pictures speak for you, or to provide fodder for clever headlines and puns. Fail to think visually and you cut yourself off from all of this, leaving your work potentially flat and one-dimensional.

Make the most of words

Design need not rely on pictures. Sometimes words on their own can have huge impact. Copywriters and designers can use a variety of graphological devices to draw attention to words, giving them added emphasis.

Repeated letters

In radio and TV ads, repeated sounds can be used to attract attention. In print, create that effect by repeating letters. You can emphasise particular letters in a variety of ways.

Enlargement

An ad to promote a luxurious cruise liner, the SS Steamer, could do this:

SSuperior SSpecial SSumptuous
SSail with the SS SSteamer

The designer could produce artwork showing the 'SS' letters in the same colours and logotype as the SS Steamer, thus visually reinforcing the written message.

Capitalisation

A company wanted to show its expertise in information technology (IT). A series of ads featured various benefits offered by the company. Each showed a one-word benefit in which the letters 'IT' appeared in upper case, such as productivITy, followed by a strapline. By capitalising the key letters, it was possible to convey two messages using just one word. A garage offering MOTs could use the same device:

MOTorist MOTorway
Get in MOTion
Get your MOT at MOTability

One letter, several slots

Take a principal letter and use clever layout so that that one letter fills several slots:

Tobin's Teacakes
Put the T into Teatime

T a s t i e s T o b i n ' s
e
a
c
a
k
e
s

This fictitious example works at a number of levels. The slogan 'Put the T into Teatime' is reinforced by the use of the letter 'T', which is reproduced in the same font. Even the text is T-shaped. It's not wonderful copy when read aloud, but as a designed advert it is effective.

Uncommon letters

Use uncommon letters to draw attention to your copy. As you skim-read copy, uncommon letters ('x', 'q', 'z', 'j' and 'k') leap out. The most common letter in English is 'e', followed by 't', 'a', 'i' and 's'. For obvious reasons, it can be tricky to write copy that uses uncommon letters. One way to use them is to spell ordinary words in a different way: stax rather than stacks, loox not looks, cheeze not cheese. As these words sound the same, this treatment is unsuitable for radio advertising, but can work with written copy.

tip

The less common letters are those which tend to attract the higher scores in the word game Scrabble. Start looking out for them.

If you were advertising a brand of cheese called Cheezz, you could play up the use of the letter 'z'.

> *If your cheese is boring . . . z z z z z z z z z*
> *Try our Cheezz*

Here 'z' is used to suggest snoring, implying that its rivals are dull.

Be careful with this technique, as it can sometimes look a little downmarket and cringe-making. How often have you seen shops called Krazy Kutz or Kwik something or other?

Of the uncommon letters, 'x' is the most popular. A one-minute brainstorm of product names produced: Dettox, Dulux, Durex, Tippex, Kleenex, Rolex, Radox, Biotex, Copydex, OXO, Sandtex, Moulinex, Exlax and Zovirax. See what you can add to the list.

TRUE STORY

Heinz uses this technique in its famous 'Beanz Meanz Heinz' slogan. Read aloud, the slogan features rhyme and assonance. In print, repetition of the 'z' combined with the fact that 'z' is an uncommon letter, plus the unusual spelling (beanz meanz), all serve to attract attention.

Onomatopoeia

Change the spelling of a word so that it becomes onomatopoeic. Onomatopoeia is the naming of a thing or action by a vocal imitation of the sound associated with it, such as 'whip', 'clang', 'sizzle' or 'buzz'. Panasonic's hiss-free cordless phone was advertised like this:

> *Introducing a cordless telephone with something missssing*

Splitting words

A word technique that relies on design for its effect is the practice of breaking or splitting a word or words into new combinations. Take this ad for low-fat sunflower margarine:

SUNF
   LOWER

You need to look twice to work it out. When you do, you see that it's a sunflower spread that is lower in fat. It says a lot in just one word, and it engages the reader in interpreting its meaning. Neat!

Here's another example, also for a spread, which uses the technique in a different way. This billboard advert shows butter melting over a close-up shot of corn on the cob. The text says:

All you need is love

On closer inspection, you see that what it actually says is:

All you need is Clover

The 'C' and 'r' in 'Clover' (the brand name for the product) are printed in green; all the rest of the text is in yellow. Design creates this double meaning, but the copywriter takes credit for producing wording that could be designed to create this effect.

The Clover ad is a visual pun. There are many examples of visual puns in marketing material. Perrier, the French mineral water bottler, produced an amusing range of adverts in the 1980s, which used 'eau' (the French word for water, pronounced 'o') in place of the letter 'o' in a variety of words.

A bottle of Perrier was headlined:

H2Eau

A modern art, cubist representation of a bottle of Perrier read:

Picasseau

These adverts were clever because:

- Copy and design worked together.
- The use of the French word 'eau' reinforced the French origin of the drink.
- The 'eau' punning was apt, since it was promoting water.
- The 'eau' sound gave the ads a French accent.
- Overall this produced witty, appealing and memorable adverts.

tip

Visit www.perrier.com to see Perrier ads over the years, including visuals from the ads referred to above.

Symbols as letters/words

Sometimes you can use an appropriate symbol in place of a letter:

SAVE MON£Y AT TOPPER'S

I L♥VE HEARTS BISTR♥

D❑N'T BE SQUARE WHEN IT C❑MES TO FASHI❑N

GET R❍UND TO SP❍OK'S B❍UTIQUE N❍W

Symbols have instant meaning. By replacing a letter with a symbol, we can reinforce our point. Use symbols to replace whole words too.

tip

Mobile phone text talk is a rich source of weird but instantly understandable word/number combos – L8 (late); 3sum (threesome); EZ (easy – works better with an American accent!) to name but three.

Letters as words/sentences

Use letters to signify a word. Lucozade ran a campaign around the letters NRG (energy). See what words and sentences you can make up. You could use XTC (ecstasy); MT (empty); XL (excel) . . . British Telecom (BT) used this technique in reverse with its Beattie (BT) character back in the 1980s, played by Maureen Lipman.

Letters and numbers

You can also mix numbers with letters to form words. Take this ludicrous example invented merely to illustrate the technique, for a fictitious company called 10–10 Tenders:

When it comes 2 10ders we have the 10acity of a K9. Heaven 4bid that anyone should undercut us on price! So if you want a competitive quote 2day, call **10–10 Tenders.**

Calligrammes

You might have used this technique at school. Typography is used to form your text into a shape which is related to the subject you are writing about. In a brochure for a garden supply company, the text may be laid out in the shape of a tree, a flower or a watering can. British Airways used this technique in press ads to publicise their new reclinable seats. Text describing other airlines' seats was laid out to look like an uncomfortable upright seat. Text describing their recliners resembled a comfortable reclining seat. By setting the text to form a shape, the message of the words was reinforced visually.

When to give more emphasis to design than copy

Sometimes photos and illustrations receive more emphasis than text. This is particularly true of advertising focusing on style and image, and publicity where a product is differentiated by its appearance (fashion clothes, jewellery or cars). It is also the case where a product is difficult to write about, such as perfume. Here, glamorous or romantic images take the place of text. Although it may pain the writer, images should always be used in place of copy if the chosen picture really can, as the saying goes, do the job of a thousand words. A photo of a child, face alight with delight as he opens his birthday presents, is probably far more compelling than a verbal description of that scene. A photo here can convey emotion more quickly, more powerfully and more effectively than words could. The same goes for diagrams and their ability to show complex information in a clear, simple and easy to understand way. Imagine trying to explain the layout of the London Underground in words!

Working with designers

To get the best out of a designer you need to let them into your head. Explain as much as you can about your copy – who it is for, what points you are trying to convey, which are the key parts. Tell them what kind of an image you are trying to create – upmarket, trendy, sophisticated, informal. Make sure they understand what you are trying to achieve.

Before giving copy to a designer, print out your work and read through it very carefully. Check:

- spelling
- punctuation
- for typos.

Typos (typographical errors) can spoil otherwise good copy and talented design.

Types of typo

- **The finger slip** – Your fingers slip on the keyboard so instead of typing 'son' you type 'aon' (the 'S' key is next to the 'A'). These are as easy to spot as they are to make, and will be detected by your word processor's spellchecker.
- **The concentration lapse** – Tired and distracted copywriters make mistakes. Errors creep in during concentration lapses. You might type 'be' for 'by', 'you' for 'your' or 'is' for 'in'. Your

spellchecker will miss these, as they are proper (albeit the wrong) words. Chances are that you'll overlook them too, because we tend to read what we think is there, not what is actually there.

- **Editing typos** – These frequently arise when you 'cut and paste' text. You may leave a straggling word behind that should have been moved or removed. Editing typos also occur when you change one part of the sentence and forget to change the rest to make sense.

> **tip**
>
> Print out your copy before proofing: it's easier to spot the mistakes on paper than on a computer screen.

Top tips for typo-spotting

- Don't scan or speed-read. Read every word, letter by letter, and every punctuation mark. Read what's there, not what you think is there.
- Read text aloud.
- Read the page from bottom to top, and even right to left, to read what's actually there (rather then what you expect to see there).
- Ask someone else to help spot what you missed!

What to look out for

- **Repeated words** – 'We went to to the park'.
- **Spelling mistakes** – 'accomodation'.
- **Correct words in the wrong place** – 'They went on there own.' Spellchecker will miss these mistakes.
- **Missed words** – 'We went the park'.
- **Words with two spellings** – 'co-ordinate' and 'coordinate'. Be consistent.
- **Consistency of 'ise' endings** – as in 'utilise' (UK), or 'ize' as in 'utilize' (US).

Checking what comes back

Hand over perfect text to your designer, and check just as carefully what you get back. Errors can creep in at design stage. Look over the designed proofs and check that the designer has given the right prominence to your words. Perhaps they have emphasised a section of text that is not all that important, or ignored one that is. Maybe they have treated your subheads as main headings. Check everything and ensure it's correct.

What to check

- Maps, pie charts, diagrams – ensure they show correct locations, proportions and legends.
- Number sequence – for footnotes and pages

- Numbers in telephone numbers, charts etc.
- Photos and captions – for correct pairing.
- Quotation marks and parentheses (brackets) for pairing.
- Ensure that main headings appear as main headings, subheadings as subheadings etc.
- Ensure consistency of fonts, pointsizes etc.
- Check for spelling mistakes in captions and headlines.
- Compare your original text against the proof. Look out for missing sections.
- Incorrect line breaks.
- Awkward word and page breaks.

tip

On seeing your copy designed, you may want to revisit the text to make some edits that will enhance the design. If your copy is slightly too long (by just two or three words), forcing your designer to start a new page, perhaps you can edit to help it fit the allocated space. Sometimes you can gain a whole line by deleting or shortening just one word.

Have a go yourself

Proofreading test

Put your proofreading skills to the test. Circle all of the errors in the following piece of copy. Then go back and correct them.

PROOFREADING MADE EASY

Its not difficult to proof read, though it does take time, patience and an eagle eye. All to often misstakes are made. Some-times a word missed out. Or maybe a necesary peice of text is omited. You're job as proof-reader is is too spot mistakes and insure they are correctted. you must also look out for words that are mispelled. Frequently words like accomodation, publically, vaccuum and goverment are spelt incorrectly. Every libary has a supply of good dictionary, so theres no excuse. Every organisation should aim for excelence in it's publicity. Instal appropriat systems to gaurd against the likelyhood of of errors.

Answers

There were 32 errors. Did you spot them all? Not such a good proofreader as you thought? If you missed anything, or got it wrong, you will need to brush up your proofreading skills. Remember that mistakes in your materials could cost you your reputation.

The text from the test is reproduced below. Mistakes are in bold, with the correction alongside in square brackets.

PROOFREADING MADE EASY

Its [It's] not difficult to **proof read** [proofread], though it does take time, patience and an eagle eye. All **to** [too] often **misstakes** [mistakes] are made. **Some-times** [Sometimes] a word [is] missed out. Or maybe a **necesary** [necessary] **peice** [piece] of text is **omited** [omitted]. **You're** [Your] job as **proof-reader** [proofreader] is **is** [delete] **too** [to] spot mistakes and **insure** [ensure] they are **correctted** [corrected]. **you** [You] must also look out for words that are **mispelled** [misspelled]. Frequently words **like** [too many spaces after this word] **accomodation** [accommodation], **publically** [publicly], **vaccuum** [vacuum] and **goverment** [government] are spelt incorrectly. Every **libary** [library] has a supply of good **dictionary** [dictionaries], so **theres** [there's] no excuse. Every organisation should aim for **excelence** [excellence] in **it's** [its] publicity. **Instal** [Install] **appropriat** [appropriate] systems to **gaurd** [guard] against the **likelyhood** [likelihood] of **of** [delete] errors.

PART TWO

This section explains how to approach the main pieces of work you are likely to have to produce – from news releases and newsletters to direct mail and adverts. Each chapter shows step-by-step how to do it, with helpful tips and advice.

Direct mail

This chapter looks at the complete direct mail package, starting with the envelope and going through to the covering letter and any enclosures. Find out how to produce powerful packages to help you sell through the letterbox.

Direct mail acquired the derisory term 'junk mail' because much of it was (and sometimes still is) badly targeted and poorly written. Since our subject is writing, not marketing, we will stick to the copy aspect of direct mail. But remember that wonderful words will fail to sell if you send them to the wrong people. Good copywriting is a partner in successful direct mail, effective only if combined with accurate targeting.

Readers will take the following steps if you have produced a well-composed, tightly targeted mailshot.

1. They will look at and then open the envelope.
2. They will read the contents.
3. They will place an order (or take some other desired action).

The steps are taken in that sequence. A reader cannot place an order until they have opened the envelope and read the mailing. Your first task as copywriter is to get the envelope opened. We all open our personal mail (what little we receive these days). A pastel pink envelope bearing cousin Susan's distinctive handwriting will be eagerly opened and its contents devoured. But a pile of unsolicited 'junk' mail? That's another matter!

Senders of mass mailings use all kinds of tricks – from mock handwriting to personalisation – but you know that it's nothing more than a computer-generated mailshot being sent to thousands or millions of others too. What do you do with it? Bin it unopened?

Take a quick look and then bin it? Or keenly tear it open, read all the contents, and place an order straight away? How your reader reacts is down to you – and the care you have taken.

The envelope

Let's start with the outside of your mailshot: the envelope. This is what the recipient sees first. Fail here and your prospect will not open it. If they don't open it, they can't read its contents and can't place an order/support your cause/join your organisation. Your hard work will be consigned to the waste paper basket. So think of the envelope not as just a carrier for your mailing, but as an integral part of the package. It can make the difference between a mailing being opened or trashed.

Choose from plain white or manila envelopes for mailshots, or have envelopes custom-made and printed with your message. With the printed option, think carefully about the envelope's copy and design. This is every bit as important as writing the enclosures.

Most printed envelopes carry a message designed to attract the reader and encourage them to open the mailing. You can take three approaches:

- **Urgent** – Urgency encourages action. Use words likely to create a sense of urgency, such as: 'Open **now** to save £20 on your membership renewal' or 'We've got great offers inside, but **hurry** – stocks are limited'.
- **Teasing** – Envelope teasers can capture the imagination and encourage the recipient to open the mailing. A cryptic message like 'A singing dog' could be bizarre enough to get your reader reaching for their letter opener.
- **Incomplete** – Start a sentence on the envelope and complete it in the headline of your enclosure. Use the envelope to get the reader reading your letter. Your envelope might say: 'The holiday of your dreams . . .' and the covering letter continue with '. . . is yours for just £5 a week.'

You can also use envelope messages to convey information:

- **Informative** – An informative statement printed on an envelope enables you to get a message across even if the envelope is never opened. A slogan such as 'Birmingham's Number One Gents' Outfitter' printed boldly across an envelope, along with a logo and address, could influence the recipient at some later date, even if they fail to open to this particular mailing. It's important awareness-building.

Any message on the envelope must link with the covering letter. If your envelope says:

> **tip**
>
> Do not use the 'incomplete' technique for business mailings: often secretaries open mail and discard envelopes before passing the contents on to the addressee.

'Bald? We can restore your hair!'

then the headline of your covering letter should say:

One Hirsute Pill each day transforms bald heads into crowning glories.

The enclosures

Most mailings comprise a covering letter and one or more enclosures. The enclosures may be:

- a mail order catalogue*
- an order form
- a reply card*
- a leaflet*
- a questionnaire
- a newsletter*
- a product sample
- a brochure
- a money-off voucher
- a pre-paid envelope

* You can read more about these elsewhere in this book.

Whatever other enclosures are contained in your mailing, at least one is likely to be the covering letter.

The covering letter

If there are other enclosures, the covering letter acts as navigator, explaining to your readers what else is enclosed and why. It guides them through the mailing and leads them to take the necessary action. If the letter itself is the only enclosure, it becomes more important still. This is your one chance. There's no glossy brochure or free sample to back you up.

Use the covering letter to capture the recipient's interest – immediately. Fail to engage them straight away and you can just pack up and go home. They will not read on in the hope of finding something interesting a few paragraphs later. No. They will give up. Goodbye order, hello dustbin.

Your covering letter will be one of the following:

- **Sales** – These are letters that are designed to sell there and then (by getting the recipient to place an order).
- **Lead-generating** – Unlike sales letters, these aim to get the recipient to express an interest. You then follow up with a further mailing, phone call or a visit.

- **Information** – You might be writing to inform customers about price increases, changes to your service or to remind them that their membership renewal is due.
- **Navigational** – This type of letter steers your reader through the mailing, summarising what's in it and what's on offer. Navigational letters can also double up as information, sales or lead-generating letters.

Sales Letters

Selling by letter is very different from selling face-to-face, something which must be borne in mind when writing a sales letter. Some copywriters lead in too gradually. They begin with the background information, progress through the letter to cover the detail, then end with the offer. This is a clear and logical way to write – if you are sure your reader will sit down and read through your letter from start to finish. They won't! So turn logic on its head. Engage the reader right from the start. Hook them by explaining upfront that you can help them save money, save the planet, save lives, be sexier, attain eternal youth, climb the career ladder . . . or whatever. Then go on to explain how.

Hooks to Hook 'em

Like fishing, there are various hooks you can use to catch your reader.

- **The 'sit up and take notice' statement** – 'There are only four pairs of gazebo monkeys left on the planet'.
- **The amazing fact** – 'Half of the water destined for your houses never gets there – it's lost through cracked pipes'.
- **The question you can't ignore** – 'Want to cut your heating bills?' or 'How would you cope if you lost your job today?'
- **The real life story** – 'Mandy is seven and suffers from Battens Disease. Few children with the condition live beyond eight . . .'
- **The direct comparison** – 'Jenny James is about the same age as you, but she looks years younger. How? Because she uses . . .'
- **The fantastic offer** – 'We're the best bank in town – or your money back'.
- **The incentive** – 'You could win a fabulous family holiday in Florida'.
- **The trip down 'Memory Lane'** – 'The Kings Road was buzzing, flower power was the rage, ethnic fashions were in, and life had never been better. Our 'Hits of the '60s' CDs really capture the mood of the decade . . .'
- **The endorsement** – 'The Viking, The Grant Arms, The Green Man, The King's Head – which is the odd one out? You are. They already use Freeman's frozen meals to help them provide the best bar meals in town . . .'

- **The testimonial** – 'Since attending Jack French's public speaking seminar, my confidence has grown 500%. I would have no qualms whatsoever in standing up and talking to 1,000 people.' What could a Jack French seminar do for your confidence?'
- **Strength in numbers** – 'Two million Scots shop at QuickMark. Do you?'
- **Reappraisal** – 'Think you can't afford a conservatory like this? Think again!'
- **Test results** – 'Recent surveys by independent motoring organisations revealed that our car servicing is the most comprehensive and affordable in . . .'

These openers are irresistible. The reader wants to know more. You've hooked them. Now lead on with your offer or proposition. How you present this is vital. Remember that no one buys products or services *per se*: we buy solutions to problems. So if you want to write a sales letter that sells, address that problem and offer the solution. That way you will be communicating in a meaningful and relevant way with your readers.

Think carefully about how you word your deal. Don't just state the price; emphasise the value. Don't write:

☒ *5 reams of recycled A4 paper for just £15 from Poppington's Paper*

write:

☑ *Buy direct and save! 5 reams of quality recycled A4 paper delivered direct to your office for just £15. Why pay more!*

If it is a good deal, make it sound that way. Spell it out. Don't assume the reader will know it's a great offer. Your words can have a measurable effect on the bottom line: your organisation's success.

TRUE STORY

A book club offered two books for the price of one. They discovered that the same offer, worded differently ('buy one, get one free'), was far more effective.

Other research has shown that 'buy one, get one free' is more powerful than '50% off'. So word your offer for maximum attraction.

Top tips for sales letters

- Where possible, give a 'get out clause' to reassure readers that you are genuine and *bona fide*. This can be as simple as: 'Return your goods to us within 10 days if you are not completely satisfied and we will give you a full, no-quibble refund'.

- Highlight any guarantees you offer.
- Spell out clearly what the reader needs to do to take up your offer – 'Visit our showroom before the end of June' or 'return the tear-off slip within the next seven days'.
- Set a deadline to create a sense of urgency and prompt an immediate response. 'Hurry. Offer ends on January 31st' is better than 'Take advantage of this special offer now'.
- Make it easy for readers to respond – enclose a return envelope with a stamp or an easy-to-complete coupon, include your telephone number or website address. (Further ideas on making it easy to respond can be found later in this chapter.)

The Five Ps

Keep sales letters:

- **Punchy** – By keeping to one side of paper. If you go onto two sides, end page one with a split sentence to encourage the reader to turn the page. (It's OK for enclosures to be lengthy, but keep your letter to the point.)
- **Personal** – Write in the first person. Be natural and use everyday words. Use a style appropriate for the audience and the subject matter.
- **Persuasive** – Put forward powerful reasons why they should buy the product/join up/support you/use the service.
- **Pulling** – Make sure everything about the package has pulling power, attracting the reader and keeping them.
- **Pushing** – Gently push the reader in the right direction, so that they place an order or return a coupon for more information.

Ensure your letter has:

- **A beginning** – The hook.
- **A middle** – The facts/detail/proposition (briefly!)
- **An end** – The action required or a response device.
- **A postscript** – This is optional. A hand-written style PS stands out from the rest of the text and can be used to reinforce the offer or encourage action: 'Hurry – offer only available until . . .' or 'Remember, we cannot repeat this offer at these spectacular prices, so order today . . .'

Lead-generating letters

A sales letter should generate sales as a result of the letter; a lead-generating letter aims to create a list of strong leads. It weeds out those who are not serious buyers, leaving you with genuine prospects to woo. Lead-generating letters are the first step in the sales process, requiring follow-up in the form of other letters, further information, samples, a telephone call, or some other method.

Be clear on whether you are writing a sales letter or a lead-generating one. Lead-generating letters should be fairly short. Don't go into too much detail at this stage: all you are doing is asking someone to show an interest; you are not trying to sell just yet. Many of the rules relating to sales letters also apply to the lead-generating variety.

Information letters

These letters must flag up at the start what their purpose is.

URGENT SAFETY NOTICE: MCSWEENEY PUSHCHAIRS

IMPORTANT CHANGE TO BILLING ARRANGEMENTS

MEMBERSHIP RENEWAL OVERDUE

Then go on to give the detailed information. Spell out what action is required:

Return your pushchair immediately to any McSweeney store, where we will fit new safety nuts free of charge.

Complete the enclosed direct debit form and return it to your bank by 1st September so that the new billing arrangements can be put in place.

Navigational letters

Navigational letters should be short and clear, with lots of bullet points:

Thanks for your enquiry about Duson Paints. We enclose:

- *A colour card showing our range of 200+ paints.*
- *A decorating tips leaflet.*
- *A brochure containing creative yet easy-to-achieve ideas for using colour in your home.*
- *A money-off voucher.*
- *A list of local stockists.*

If you would like to know anything more about Duson Paints . . .

Their aim is to hold a mailing together, to explain what is in it, and to signpost readers to the enclosure(s).

Easy action

Your ultimate success depends on the ease with which you enable people to respond to your mailing. Use a combination from the list below to ensure that action is easy:

- **Response mechanism** – Include an order form, a simple tear-off slip, a coupon/card to allow easy response.
- **Business reply** – Paying the postage for your customer's reply increases response. Envelopes or cards pre-printed with your address make it easy for recipients to respond.
- **Freepost** – Your enquirers/respondents can write to you post-free, though you will have to pick up the tab. Some charities include a Freepost address, but point out that you can help the charity by paying your own postage.
- **Freephone** – Freephone and 'lo-call' numbers can boost the response. Research shows that people generally prefer to respond by post rather than by telephone.
- **Credit card payment** – If people are able to pay by credit card, it is even easier for them to respond. A Freephone credit card hotline makes it easier still.

Encourage responses by including a 'speed incentive':
Reply by June 30th and we'll knock 10% off your bill.

Targeting

Wherever possible, write for a tight audience. The clearer the audience, the better targeted the messages. Unlike an expensive brochure, letters can be tailored to the audience in half a dozen completely different versions for little or no extra cost. It means that you can send out the same mailshot, but with a different covering letter, to:

- existing customers/donors/supporters
- cold prospects
- warm prospects.

Reply cards

Many direct mail packages include a reply card, providing the recipient with an easy way to seek further information. Reply cards are often left until last and written hurriedly with little thought because they are regarded as simply a way of capturing interested readers' details. They are more than that. The reply card is a valuable opportunity to restate your offer and reinforce your message. You're missing a trick if you use it simply to build up a mailing list of warm prospects. The reply card needs to be copywritten because it is an important selling opportunity. It should look something like this:

> *Please send me your FREE information guide to installing a new bathroom, full of great tips and stylish ideas. I understand that I am under NO OBLIGATION to buy, but if I place an order in the next two months I will qualify for a 10% discount.*

The reply card allows you to briefly restate your case. Don't use it just to collect names and addresses; really get it working for you.

tip

Direct mail provides the perfect way to test your copy. Systematically change various elements of your copy, and monitor the responses to the mailings to test the effectiveness of different approaches. Use it to discover what sort of headline, envelope or body copy produces the best results. Do you get a better response with short or longer copy? Does an envelope with a printed message make a difference to the quantity and quality of responses? A test mailing could help you find out. Don't introduce more than one variable in each test or you will not know which factor led to increased or decreased response.

Advertising

This chapter explains how we read adverts and shows how to write them. Take a close look at the various components of an ad, such as the headline and the body text, and discover what role each plays in an effective advert.

Advertising executives are the most envied of marketing professionals. They get to deal with big budgets and prestigious assignments, to work with the stars and parade their work for the world to admire. True? Most people who work in advertising would not recognise this description. Aside from the top end, advertising is less glamorous than you might expect, so don't let the aura surrounding it put you off trying to write advertising copy.

Before you put pen to paper, do your homework.

- **Understand your audience** – To communicate effectively you need to know who you are writing for.
- **Know the competition** – If you know what they are offering, you can offer something better, or differentiate yourself in some other way.
- **Know your UBP** – Your Unique Buying Point. This is different from a USP (Unique Selling Point – see page 15); it focuses on what counts for the buyer. USPs are product-centred.
- **Know your benefits** – You will know from Chapter 2 that you should sell benefits, not features (see page 14).

AIDA

Good advertising should employ the AIDA formula. AIDA is an acronym standing for Attention, Interest, Desire and Action.

- Your advert will be competing with many others, so it must stand out and attract **Attention** if you want it noticed (a vital precursor to its being read).
- It must engage the reader's **Interest** so that they will keep reading (or listening or watching). If you cannot maintain interest, you will lose your readers long before you have convinced them to buy.
- It should stimulate **Desire** – to buy your products or use your service.
- It must prompt **Action**. What use is an arresting ad that encourages interest and desire, if no action results? Your advert must make it easy for readers/listeners to take the necessary action.

Attention

For print ads (radio adverts come later in this chapter), strong photographs, bold design, bright colours (or striking use of black and white in a colour publication), or a combination of these can help achieve something that gets noticed. That's your designer's job. From the copy side, arresting headlines can be effective attention-grabbers. Read how to write a powerful headline later in this chapter.

Topical references provide another technique for attracting attention. During a national postal strike, an internet service provider placed the following press advert:

TODAY IT'S E-MAIL OR NO MAIL . . . We'd like to thank today's striking postal workers for the opportunity to bring the cause of e-mail to the notice of the British public. There's not much to say about e-mail except that it's faster, cheaper and more flexible than ordinary mail . . . Oh, and it never goes on strike.

In the run-up to National Tyre Safety Week Kwik-Fit ran this ad:

SOMEONE WILL PROBABLY CHECK YOUR TYRES NEXT WEEK. MAKE SURE IT'S OUR BOYS IN BLUE.

Next week . . . police will be stopping cars to check the condition of their tyres. If you are found to have tyres that are . . . you could be fined up to £2,500 and 3 penalty points for EACH tyre. Call Kwik-Fit first. We'll give you a free report . . .

The topical link makes the adverts more relevant and therefore more likely to be read.

Interest

Attract the reader's interest, then hold it. You'll lose readers with over-long copy, complicated messages, or pompous/obscure language. Keep copy lively and your message simple yet interesting.

Desire

Use copy to make your reader want (really, really want!) what you're offering. Get them longing to save the otter from extinction, craving for a cleaner toilet or desperate for that soft lambswool jumper you're selling.

Action

Action is the acid test of an ad's effectiveness. Some award-winning ads are high on style, low on action. However great your advert looks, or however beautifully it reads, it is worthless if it fails to achieve a sale. Spell out what action is required, prompt readers to take it, and enable them to do so with ease.

Be clear on what action you want readers to take. Do you want them to:

- Visit your store/outlet/service?
- Place an order/take out a subscription?
- Ask you for a quotation for work?
- Complete a coupon requesting more information or a free publicity or campaign pack?
- Send for a free sample?
- Visit your website?
- Call you for details of a product or service?
- Take out membership or send in a donation?
- Change their buying behaviour (by switching to your product)?

Look at your completed advert and ask yourself: 'Is it clear what the reader has to do? Have I made it easy for them?' Pay attention to what you are asking your reader to do, and ensure you are specific about what action is required. Never use a vague expression like:

☒ *We hope to hear from you soon*

Be specific and directive:

☑ *Return this coupon today*
☑ *Contact us before July 1st to take advantage of this great offer*

How we 'read' adverts

Research in how we read ads has shown that there is a definite route, or 'eye path,' which we follow on first seeing an advert.

1. **Picture** – We look at this first.
2. **Headline** – Then we move to the headline, where 80% of readers give up.

3. **Bottom right-hand corner** – Those still reading move here next. Most advertisers place their name and logo in this spot. Few readers will go further than this.
4. **Caption** – The caption on the photo or illustration is the bit read next.
5. **Cross heading** – Next readers scan the cross headings, sub-headings, other illustrations and graphs.
6. **Body text** – Last of all readers go to the 'body text', the main part of your advert.

Put all your effort into the body text and you'll be ignoring the massive 80+% of readers who never get this far! The lesson is simple: do not rely on body text. If your picture and headline fail to attract, you might as well not bother with body copy.

Pictures plus headlines

As your picture and headline are readers' first ports of call, they must be given special attention. The headline should not simply state what the picture shows. It needs to work harder than that. Each needs the other to make sense. Together they should produce a powerful message that is more than the sum of the individual parts.

Not every advert needs a photograph or illustration, but each should have a headline. Only one in five will read beyond it, so use it well.

Headlines

The function of the headline is to:

- create an immediate impact;
- attract attention;
- attract the right prospects;
- lure readers into reading your body text.

There are various types of headline:

- direct
- indirect
- 'how to'
- questions
- commands.

Direct headlines

These headlines get straight to the point:

Cheddar. Only £1 a 1lb at Sainsway

Your £50 donation can support a child through school for a whole year

OVER 500 USED CARS AT EVERY PITSTOP SHOWROOM

The strength of these headlines is that they communicate a complete message. Their drawback is that they are so complete as to make it unnecessary for the reader to delve into the body text. Write direct headlines that also lead the reader into the copy. Look at the above. Now see how a little rewriting can lead readers from headline to text.

How Sainsway can sell cheddar at only £1 a 1lb
Our competitors will charge you twice this. Because we cut back on the fripperies – fancy in-store displays, expensive promotion and packaging . . . we can give you top quality products at bargain basement prices. Lower overheads mean lower prices.

How your £50 donation can support a child through school for a whole year
It's only £50 to you, but it's 12 months of life-changing education to a child in Ecuador.

How can Pitstop Showrooms guarantee you a selection of over 500 used cars?
Easy. As the top name dealer in used cars, we have the resources to carry a huge stock. That means more choice for you, and better value too.

Now you have direct headlines that are strong in their own right, which also encourage the reader to find out more. Direct headlines can also be used to attract the right prospects:

CALLING ALL MUMS AND DADS
Cheap ways to keep your kids occupied this summer

ADDICTED TO GAMBLING?
Our helpline has supported hundreds of people in your position. Let us help you put your life back together.

Paying too much for your petrol?

Body text is not compulsory. Stand-alone headlines can do the job too:

London to Manchester only £20 return by rail

Indirect headlines

Indirect headlines attract interest and curiosity, but require the right body copy to make any sense:

PURE HEAVEN

This headline might attract attention, but what does it mean? You need to read the rest of the advert to find out:

PURE HEAVEN
ZZ-Beds are so comfortable that we guarantee you the deepest, longest and purest sleep you've ever had. It's the closest you will get to heaven on earth.

'How to' headlines

These headlines do what they say:

How to choose a new vacuum cleaner

How to quit smoking

You need not spell out the 'how to' bit. You can just imply it:

Crisp chips – without a deep fat fryer

Effectively this headline is saying: 'How to get crisp chips without a deep fat fryer'.

Question headlines

Phrase your question in such a way as to demand an answer:

Do you want to preserve beautiful historic buildings for the next generation?

Sometimes you can ask a question without asking a question:

Why mums prefer Poopers Nappies

Strictly speaking this is not a question, but effectively it is the question: 'Would you like to know why mothers prefer Poopers

tip

Headlines that
offer the promise
of a reward
attract more
attention. The
reward need not
be of the 'buy
one get one free'
type, where you
are offering a
genuine financial
reward. It can be
a promise: 'Sleep
easy tonight' for
example.

Nappies?'. The addition of 'why' makes your readers curious.
'Mothers prefer Poopers Nappies' is more likely to leave readers
thinking 'so what?'

Command headlines

These headlines (politely) instruct the reader:

> *Cut out the coupon. Cut out the middleman*
>
> *Be careful. Fireworks can kill*

Subheadings

Sometimes the main headline has a subordinate headline immediately
below it:

BONZO'S OWNERS DUMPED HIM IN A LAYBY ON THE M6

*You can give him, or one of his 300 doggy pals at Muts' Rescue, a loving
home*

Subheads help you expand on the point of the main headline, adding
more information or detail – but not so much that the subhead
becomes body text.

The body text

Although 80% of readers will not get this far, that's no excuse to
pay body text less attention. Those reading it have shown by their
perseverance that they are interested in what you have to say.

Body text types

- **Reason-why** – This is where you make a statement and proceed
  to explain or justify it, offering reasons that appeal to logic.
  Essentially you are telling your reader why they should buy your
  product/use your service/support your cause:

  THE BEST PEAS IN THE WORLD
  *That's quite a claim, but who else can match our standards? Delicious
  organically grown Fair Trade peas, specially selected for flavour and
  bite. Each pea is inspected for quality and freshness, and we think nothing
  of rejecting up to 60% . . .*

- **Descriptive** – This kind of copy can be dull. It simply describes
  a product or service.

BODY TEXT DOS AND DON'TS

DO

☑ Explain your headline.

☑ Explain your photo/illustration, if you used one.

☑ Give more detail.

☑ Offer compelling facts and information.

☑ Draw the reader in and keep them hooked.

DON'T

☒ Waffle.

☒ Try to say too much.

☒ Use the third person.

☒ Present too many ideas or propositions.

☒ Use too much unbroken text or small print.

- **Humour** – This kind of copy can be so effective, but you need to be truly funny for it to work. Humorous copy is the most difficult for a novice to write effectively and as humour is so subjective, any misjudgement may end up offending some readers.
- **Testimonial** – This is where someone testifies to a product's quality, value or features.

Captions

Failure to caption photos, graphs and other illustrations is a missed opportunity. Captions attract twice the readership of your body text, so they provide a prime opportunity to communicate your message. Be creative with captions. Never simply state what is in the picture: add to it.

☒ *Adanna at school*

☑ *School has opened Adanna's horizons and will provide her with the skills to help others in her village*

Dominance of design

There was a time when the copywriter was king. Think back to old editions of *The Times*, where adverts were entirely text-based. Look

> **tip**
>
> Short copy is generally better, so long as it contains all the information readers want and need. But don't make it brief if that means leaving out a mass of information that is required by the reader before they will be willing to take any action.

at the ads in *The Times* today. Increasingly the role of copywriter is being undermined by the emphasis on design in advertising. Images are frequently more important than text. Some ads feature no text at all. As a copywriter, be aware of trends in advertising but don't feel threatened by them. Even if an ad comprises just a couple of words, dwarfed by a huge illustration, the copywriter had to demonstrate enormous skill in selecting those two very important words.

Classifieds

Classified ads require a completely different style to display ads. (Classifieds are small ads comprising lines of text with no design element. They are grouped by subject – Restaurants, Talks, Pets, Plumbers. Generally you pay by the line, so words are at a premium.) Remember to:

- abbreviate ('des res', not 'desirable residence; 'b&w' for 'black and white');
- omit certain words (don't bother with 'a', 'the', 'is' etc.);
- ditch complete sentences.

[x] *There will be a charity sale of bric-a-brac, to be held in Anytown church hall. It will take place on Monday, July 10th at 5.30pm. Tea, coffee and light refreshments will be served. Anyone may attend. [36 words]*

Write:

[✓] ***Charity Bric-a-Brac Sale.*** *Anytown church hall. July 10th. 5.30pm. Refreshments. All welcome. [12 words]*

While just a third as long, the second is as effective as the first and so much cheaper!

As well as lineage adverts (like the one above) there are display classifieds. Many organisations miss an opportunity by leading with their organisation's name:

CITY DOG HOME
30 Castle Street
Jacksonville
(01441) 433521
Help us help dogs in distress. Make a donation today.

JO JO'S BISTRO
37 High Street
Jacksonville
(01441) 344351
Scrummy Cajun cooking and affordable prices.

Small ads must still follow the rules of big adverts. With a simple rejigging see how much more effective they are now:

HELP US HELP DOGS IN DISTRESS
City Dog Home
30 Castle Street
Jacksonville
(01441) 433521
Make a donation today.

Scrummy Cajun cooking and affordable prices
Jo Jo's Bistro
37 High Street
Jacksonville
(01441) 344351

The copy is identical but the order has been altered, ensuring that the ads attract that all-important attention through a powerful headline.

Keep it legal

All advertising must be legal, decent, honest and truthful. The Advertising Standards Authority (ASA) investigates complaints about advertisements and ensures that advertising meets the standard and is in the public interest. For the latest version of the British Code of Advertising, Sales Promotion and Direct Marketing, visit the ASA's website – www.asa.org.uk.

The Codes apply to adverts in newspapers, magazines, catalogues, mailings, brochures and posters, but not to broadcast commercials on TV and radio. These are governed by the Broadcast Advertising Codes, which are spilt into radio and TV and are available to download from the ASA's website. The Broadcast Codes contain separate sections on charity advertising and political and controversial advertising.

TRUE STORY

In 2006 the ASA launched its first radio campaign with what it described as 'the worst advertisements ever'. The deliberately bad ads stated that while the ASA might not be able to make good ads, it can remove ads that are offensive, harmful or misleading. Each ad was deliberately unprofessional – one was full of mispronunciations, another poorly edited, and in the third the presenter was interrupted by an invitation to play golf with a friend – but the overall comic effect was designed to help convey a serious message: that the ASA exists to keep advertising standards high. Listen to the ads on the ASA'a website.

The main points to bear in mind are:

1. Adverts must be legal, decent, honest and truthful.
2. Ads should be prepared with a sense of responsibility to consumers and society.
3. Advertisers must hold documentary evidence to prove all claims are capable of objective substantiation.
4. Where there is a significant division of informed opinion about any claims made, they should not be portrayed as universally agreed.
5. No ad should cause fear or distress without good reason. Advertisers should not use shocking claims or images merely to attract attention.

It has been suggested that we see up to 2,000 sales messages every day, on TV, buses, the internet, posters and so on. We remember only about seven: the other 1,993 just pass us by! Try to get your ads into the memorable category.

Bus adverts

There are two types of bus adverts: internals and externals. External advertising must be short and simple. You are advertising on a moving vehicle to people on the move. If you have too much copy, it will be impossible to read. A short statement or headline, combined if necessary with a grabbing graphic, is sufficient. Forget cramming in everything about your product or service. Develop a clear and simple message and stick with it.

Internal advertising can be more expansive. People with time to kill – those sitting on buses – will read them. You can go into a bit more detail, but remember that you are limited by space, and your text must be large enough to be seen across the bus.

Radio ads

Radio ads are a superb vehicle for creative writers. Radio allows you to do almost anything, like visiting far-off or remote places or doing impossible things (such as going back in time). Because you are relying on sound effects, not special (and expensive) visual effects, you can do so much more. But the drawback is that you can neither show the product nor phone numbers, addresses or the 'small print'. Write to be heard, not seen.

Your initial challenge with a radio ad is to attract attention. Stand out from the other ads in the commercial break by sounding different to them – either through the way you have written your copy, the way it is read, or any sound effects used.

The average commercial is 30 seconds, which gives you around 70 words. It's not a lot, especially as you are relying on sound, with no pictures to back you up. Use sound to the full, letting it enhance your script.

tip

> Ensure your ad talks directly to your listener, and in the same way that they would speak. To write appropriately, have a mental picture of the average listener. The radio station will be able to supply you with an accurate profile of their listeners (which may vary according to the time of day). Think about this typical listener, their likes and dislikes, and where they will be listening to your ad. (72% of listeners listen to their radios in the kitchen, but 43% of 15 to 24-year-olds listen in the bathroom. Ask the radio station for their local statistics.)

Most listeners will not be in the market for your product or service when they hear your ad – but you want them to listen all the same. If your ad makes the necessary impact, they will think about you next time they want what you are offering. To achieve this your ads should be interesting, engaging, entertaining or funny – or all of these!

Radio ads must clearly signal to the listener what action they must take. Tell them:

- where they can buy your product/use the service, or
- your web address or number to call for further information (preferably something easy to recall), and/or
- where to write to for details (addresses must be short and easy).

Writing for the web

Discover how readers read website content and find out how you can improve the ease with which people read yours. Pick up usability top tips and learn how to write effective emails.

The internet is no longer a world inhabited by 'anoraks'. Most of us surf the Net both at work or home – to shop, to find information, to play games . . . It is increasingly unusual for businesses and charities, even small ones, *not* to have a website. There are plenty out there – just take a look – but not all of them are worth looking at and fewer still are worth reading. Don't jeopardise your good image with an amateurish website.

Writing for the internet is not the same as writing for the page. Web pages are read on a computer screen and all the evidence suggests that we all read much more slowly on-screen – around 25% more slowly, in fact, than when reading the same text on the printed page. What's more, the eyestrain is greater. Remember this when you come to write material for a website.

The challenge for any writer is to hold on to the reader. That's even harder with a website. There are hundreds, thousands or millions of other websites on the same subject – all available there and then to your reader. If yours fails to work for them, they will not hesitate to go elsewhere for the information.

tip
Pick up tips by visiting award-winning sites. See how they are written and learn from them.

Providing for scanners

The biggest factor you must take into account is the fact that most people do not read web pages: they scan them looking for the information they need. Highlight key words to help the eye find the section it is searching for, but limit highlighting to key information-carrying

DOS AND DON'TS OF WEB COPY

DO

☑ Keep sentences short and simple.

☑ Break text into bite-size chunks using subheadings, bulletpoints and so forth so that your site is user-friendly for screen-fatigued surfers. Visitors are disinclined to scroll through screens that look dense. They will give up and visit a rival's site instead.

☑ Remember that up to four-fifths of people scan web pages rather than reading every word. Keep text much tighter than in conventional printed publicity so that readers can go straight to the facts or information they want.

DON'T

☒ Use long paragraphs – white space aids readability so keep paragraphs short and punchy. Make sure paragraphs are separated by a line of clear space.

☒ Use the 'third person' – talk direct to readers using words like 'we' and 'you'.

☒ Ignore the reader – think about who will visit your site and write in a suitable style.

---

words. Avoid highlighting entire sentences or long phrases: a scanning eye can only pick up two or at most three words at a time. Subheadings also help readers to reach the part of your text that they need. Keep subheadings factual and meaningful to aid this; 'clever' or cryptic subheads are not a help and if you use them you will lose readers.

☒ *More heritage? Look North!*
☑ *Our Other National Heritage Properties in the North*

Many users 'information snack' – they make short visits to websites looking for quick answers. Good intra-site navigation will help them find what they need. This is not solely a job for the techies who design your site. It's primarily your job as writer. Think about how people will move around your site and structure and write copy accordingly.

Visitors to your site will move between pages as they choose, not as you might hope or expect. Make every page independent and stand-alone; do not make assumptions about previous pages seen by them.

TRUE STORY

A study has shown that website usability was improved by 124% simply by combining concise text with a scannable layout and objective language. Researchers took a website full of marketing-speak and rewrote it so that it was more concise (reducing the copy by about half). This alone improved usability by 58%. They also produced a version of the original text that was easier to scan – using bulletpoints and other devices. This improved usability by 47%. Finally, they rewrote the text in a more neutral style, ditching the hyped or exaggerated marketing-speak. This led to a 27% improvement in usability. The researchers concluded that promotional language imposes a cognitive burden on users, who have to spend time filtering out the hyperbole to get at the facts.

Effective e-mails

E-mail is still a relatively new form of communication (although there were 2.6 trillion users at the last count!) Some people are unsure of 'netiquette'. Should e-mails be formal or informal? Are they just like electronic letters and memos, or should a different style be adopted? There are no hard and fast rules, but use commonsense.

E-MAIL DOS AND DON'TS

DO

☑ Give every e-mail an explanatory subject heading to help readers prioritise and file your e-mail.

☑ Get the tone right. It's OK to be informal when appropriate (e-mailing a close friend to arrange lunch) but informality is not usually acceptable for official/business e-mails (but is acceptable for sales/marketing e-mails).

☑ Restrict the number of recipients – it's easy to 'cc' an e-mail to hundreds of others, but that's no excuse for doing so! Copy only to people who need to know, but don't overload others and waste their time just to cover your own back. A good test is to ask yourself whether you would mail a copy to others if posting rather than e-mailing.

☑ Cover all the points when responding to e-mails – if you were asked six questions, make sure you answer all six in your reply because an incomplete response will only generate a further e-mail. Where necessary, pre-empt further new questions too.

☑ Try to keep your email brief. Detailed information can be sent as an attachment.

☑ Remember the Freedom of Information Act. If someone makes an application under the legislation, any e-mails you have written about them (even internal ones) may be available to them.

☑ Make sure you send the e-mail to the right person. It's easy to hit the wrong button, sending confidential information into the wrong hands.

DON'T

☒ Add 'Urgent' to the subject line unless the e-mail genuinely requires a quick response.

☒ Hit the 'send' button before rereading your e-mail. If necessary, edit what you have written. It's quick to e-mail something but that's no excuse for sloppiness. As a quick-check, use your spellchecker.

☒ Use the 'reply to all' option unless everyone on the original list needs to see your reply.

☒ Send confidential items through an insecure server.

☒ Use capital letters in body text. In e-mail etiquette, writing in capital letters is the equivalent of shouting. It's also harder for those with a visual impairment to read upper case lettering.

TRUE STORY

Never put anything in writing that may come back and haunt you. Remember Jo Moore, the government spindoctor? She lost her job when someone leaked an e-mail she had sent saying that 9/11 (the day the World Trade Centre in New York was destroyed by terrorists) was a good day to bury bad news. If you have written an e-mail in anger, don't hit the send button until you've calmed down and reread the e-mail. You might decide to delete it!

Beware of using humour in e-mails. The Government's Trade and Industry Department, DTI, discovered in a poll of UK workers that nearly 25% of employees had suffered crossed wires as a result of others using humour in e-mails. Quite simply they misinterpreted the message and there was embarrassment all round.

Give e-mail correspondence the same care and attention as any other written communication. Research has shown that poorly written e-mails cost the UK economy millions each year if you take into account the cost of writing them and the time wasted reading them.

News releases

This chapter explains the 'five Ws' of release-writing, the essential ingredients of a successful release. Discover how to find a news angle, and how to make your release more likely to hit the headlines.

Look at your local or a national newspaper. A high percentage of the content will be derived from news releases (sometimes known as 'press releases', though this term can upset the broadcast media). A well-composed news release based on a sound storyline stands a high chance of being picked up by a newspaper, radio or TV station. But get it wrong and your news release will end up in the bin, with the scores (in some cases, hundreds) of others that didn't make the grade that day.

What is a release?

A release is a story about your organisation, work or products/ services, written in the style of a news report. It is organised and laid out in a particular way. Here's an example:

For immediate use

Tuesday, October 28 2006

JOBS BOOST FOR WEST MIDLANDS

250 New Jobs in Baking Industry

Sitwell's Bakery has announced that it will create 250 new jobs in the West Midlands by the end of the year.

The opening of four new shops in the Birmingham area will create 100 new jobs and a further 150 jobs will be provided at the company's main bakery in Wolverhampton. Around 100 of these will be baking apprenticeships for young people, with the remaining 50 being clerical positions.

Said Maria Maitkin, Chief Executive of Sitwell's: 'At a time when other companies are laying off staff, we are delighted to have good news for unemployed people in the West Midlands. We will offer quality jobs with training and genuine prospects. This represents a real boost to the local economy and real hope to local people who are currently jobless.'

The expansion at Sitwell's has been brought about following a cash injection from investors, who recently took up a share offer which has enabled the company to invest in the latest computer-controlled baking equipment.

If the West Midlands expansion is a success, as the company predicts, further initiatives will be launched in the north of England and in Scotland, creating up to 750 further new jobs.

ends

For further information contact:

Maria Maitkin, Chief Executive 01902 212127 (office) 077 1234 177 (mobile) or David Caruthers, Head of Personnel 01902 212127 (office) 077 1234 178 (mobile)

The advantage over advertising is that a release can help you secure powerful, persuasive and free media coverage. Your copy appears as editorial, so it tends to be perceived by readers as more credible and independent than a piece of advertising. The obvious drawback is that there are no guarantees. Advertising copy appears word for word as you wrote it, on the day you want it, in the media you select. With a news release, there is no guarantee that it will appear at all, let alone that it will be reproduced in the form you would wish. It might be edited or completely rewritten.

tip

Unlike other pieces of marketing material, always write a news release in the third person.

DOS AND DON'TS OF NEWS RELEASES

DO

☑ Ensure your story is a good read, while also promoting your service/product or message.

☑ Make sure your release is newsworthy.

DON'T

☒ Oversell your product/service or use exaggerated claims and hyperbole.

☒ Offer an angle that is too blatantly commercial.

The media always receive more releases than they can use. Ensure that yours is the one that leaps out from the pile, instantly grabbing the news editor's attention and interest.

Ingredients of a successful release

- A gripping first paragraph.
- A strong news angle.
- The 'five Ws' – who, what, when, where and why.
- A quote from a named person.
- A 'Note to Editors'.
- A contact name.
- A mobile phone number.

A gripping first paragraph

The first paragraph of your news release is all-important. A busy news editor will glance at your release. They will read no further unless you have hooked them. Many releases make a common mistake: they progress logically through a story, starting with the background and building up to the news. The opposite is required. Lead with the news, then explain the background.

A strong news angle

All releases must be interesting and have genuine news value. Finding an interesting news angle can be difficult. Take the launch of a new perfume. This might be big news within the company, which has worked on its formulation for years. The company's future relies on a successful consumer launch. But what is immensely important to organisations is generally not in the least bit interesting to those outside them.

> ☒ *Harmony, makers of the world's favourite perfumes, today launches a new fragrance – Imagination.*

This approach would attract zero coverage (with the possible exception of the perfume trade press). How could the company create a buzz? It could devise some kind of event to add news value:

> ☑ *Three of the world's most beautiful women jetted into London today to become the first to wear Imagination, an exclusive perfume that ounce for ounce costs more than pure gold.*

This sort of story would attract good picture coverage and hold particular appeal for tabloid and celebrity media. Or the company could focus on some aspect of the product that is newsy:

> ☑ *Controversial avant-garde artist Damien Hirst's latest creation is guaranteed to create a stir – for being too traditional! Famous for pickled animal carcasses, the artist's newest work will soon be found on the dressing tables of respectable ladies across the country. Mr Hirst has designed the scent bottle for a new perfume, Imagination, which goes on sale today.*

Which approach the company might opt for would depend on how it wanted to position the product. To help find your newsworthy angle, ask:

- Is what we are doing the biggest or the best?
- Is it a first?
- Is it special in some way?
- What will it mean for our customers/supporters/donors?
- What will it mean for the world/country/city?
- Is there something different, unusual or even unique about it?
- Are we breaking new ground?
- Are we creating new jobs?
- Will we change the way people live or work?

The five Ws

Journalists learn that every story must cover the 'five Ws':

- **Who** – Who is doing it? (Your organisation? A celebrity? A politician?)
- **What** – What are they doing? (Launching a new product/service? Making a major announcement?)

- **When** – When are they doing it?
- **Where** – Where are they doing it?
- **Why** – Why are they doing it? (To satisfy customer demand or societal need? To become a market leader?)

Check that your release covers the five Ws, but be careful not to simply string them together to form your opening sentence. It will make for a rather dull read:

For immediate use

Monday, November 3 2006

SALE OF 1960s TOYS

Acton's Sale Rooms in High Street, Peterton, will hold an auction of 1960s toys at 2pm on Saturday November 8.

Said Jeremy Dulcie-Chives, chief auctioneer at Acton's: 'Acton's is the South West's premier auction house. We are now entering our centenary year, providing an auction service to over 100,000 people each year.'

Items on sale will include dolls, trainsets, toys and boardgames.

Viewing from 10am to 7pm all day Friday, November 7.

For more information contact:

Jeremy Dulcie-Chives, Acton's chief auctioneer
Tel. 76528 (sale rooms) or 077 223667 (mobile).

The version below is far livelier and offers more scope to editors to do an interesting feature:

For immediate use

Monday, November 3 2006

PRICEY BLONDE BOMBSHELL

TO PULL CROWDS IN PETERTON

A desirable blonde bombshell in her 40s will be star attraction at next week's auction at Acton's Sale Rooms in Peterton. The early Barbie doll is just one of the lots at the sale of 1960s collectable toys taking place in the town on Saturday (November 8).

Said Jeremy Dulcie-Chives, chief auctioneer at Acton's: 'We expect a lot of people to turn out for a good reminisce. They will see toys they have not seen since their childhood, such as Barbie, Cindy and Tressy dolls, Hornby Dublo trainsets, Thunderbirds memorabilia, and classic boardgames which have long since disappeared from the shelves of our toyshops.'

Would-be buyers will need more than Monopoly money to pay for their purchases. The original Barbie doll is expected to go under the hammer for around £500.

The auction takes place at 2pm at Acton's Sale Rooms in the High Street. Viewing from 10am to 7pm all day Friday, November 7.

ends

For more information contact:

Jeremy Dulcie-Chives, Acton's chief auctioneer
Tel. 76528 (sale rooms) or 077 223667 (mobile).

This contains the five Ws, but a lot more besides.

Quote

Newspapers like releases to include a pithy quote from a named, appropriate person. It makes their readers believe that they actually interviewed you, when really they just used your release! Quotes must be interesting and believable. Never use the quote to peddle hype and nonsense:

☒ *Joe Smith, Managing Director of Harmony Perfumes, said: 'Imagination is a sophisticated scent for sophisticated women. Anyone with style will be wearing Imagination this season'.*

Make your quote newsy and knowledgeable:

☑ *Joe Smith, Managing Director of Harmony Perfumes, said: 'There is bewildering choice in the scent market, and our research shows that consumers are looking for something that stands out. Our target woman wants a fragrance that says something about her. She is well educated, interested in the arts, and has spending power. We commissioned Damien Hirst to design our bottle because . . .'*

This quote adds something to the story; the first one is mere PR-speak.

> **tip**
>
> Write your release with editing in mind. Sometimes newspapers cut a story to fit a space. It's sensible to write your release so that it can be chopped paragraph by paragraph from the bottom up and still make sense.

tip

Fail to display a
date prominently
on your release
and it may be
assumed to be
old news.
Demonstrate that
your release is
bang up to date
by showing the
current date.

Note to editors

Some releases include an optional 'Note to Editors' at the end. Include in it background information that is useful or interesting, but not vital to the story. This helps keep your release short, but ensures that you don't leave out something that could be useful to the reporter:

Note to editors:
1. *Harmony makes 27 different fragrances, including Shame, Rebelette and Roses.*
2. *Harmony, voted Perfumier of the Year 2005, has an annual turnover of £330 million.*

A contact name

Every release should contain at least one contact person. If a journalist wants to check anything in your release, they will call one of the named contacts. Contacts should be easy to get hold of, confident about talking to the media, and fully briefed.

A mobile number

Few journalists work nine-to-five, so out-of-hours contact numbers are essential. A mobile phone number means that you can be contacted at home, or when otherwise out of the office.

News release musts

1. Keep it short: preferably one page but no more than two.
2. Avoid jargon (unless it is for the trade press), hype, clichés and unexplained abbreviations/acronyms.
3. Use clear, positive language and short words and sentences to make your release snappy.
4. Don't get carried away by detail. Concentrate on the essentials and stick to the facts.

tip

Would you send
the same direct
mail package to
hot prospects as
to cold ones?
Probably not!
Don't send the
same release to
everyone either.
Local papers'
needs are
different from
national or
trade press
requirements.
Write to appeal
to the target
group of
publications.

Looking the part

Maximise your chances of getting your release into print by making sure it looks the part:

■ Use double spacing and wide margins.
■ Keep releases single sided.
■ Use your A4 headed notepaper for the top sheet, but plain white paper for continuation sheets.

- Avoid fancy formatting. Do not underline, put words in bold, italics, capitals and so on.
- Never split a sentence from one page to the next. Ideally, don't let a paragraph continue over the page.
- Staple pages together. It's easy for paper-clipped pages to get separated in a busy newsroom.

Articles and features

Most of us will be called upon from time to time to write articles for a variety of outlets – the trade/voluntary sector press, local press, in-house journals and customer/supporter newsletters. Find out how to produce readable and interesting articles with relative ease.

Some people are anxious about article/feature-writing because of the concern that their work will be published, with their 'by-line' on it, for all the world to see. No one wants to put their name to something that they fear is no good. If you have to write a piece, make the task easier by finding out:

- **Audience** – Who you are writing for. An article aimed at mechanical engineers will be rather different from one written for people suffering from drug addiction.
- **Publication** – Will it appear in a learned journal or an informal staff newsletter?
- **Style** – In what style is the publication written? Formal? Chatty? Lots of footnotes and references? Find out.
- **Length** – It is easier to write to a certain word count than to have to drastically lengthen or shorten an article afterwards.
- **Deadline** – Do you have three weeks or just three hours to produce your copy?
- **Subject** – What are you expected to write about? Get as detailed a brief as possible.
- **Purpose** – What is the purpose of your article? Is it to entertain, to educate, to inform?
- **Context** – Will your article be one of several exploring different aspects of the same subject? If so, find out what other articles are being prepared, by whom, and on what areas.

Once you have a clear idea of what is expected of you, time for some hard graft. Remember the stages of writing? To recap:

- **Gather** any thoughts and ideas.
- **Group** or organise your ideas into themes.
- **Sequence** your themes into a logical order.
- **Write** and produce an initial draft.
- **Revise** by improving first and subsequent drafts until you are happy with your finished work.

Follow these stages when feature writing.

Ideas for openers

An article relies upon its first paragraph to hook the reader. Open with one of the following:

- **A controversial statement** – 'Murder, theft and other crimes would be drastically reduced if hard drugs were legalised . . .'
- **An amazing fact or statistic** – 'The average housecat walks roughly 12 kilometres every day . . .'
- **An interesting or moving personal story** – 'David looks like any other boy, only he's not. Unlike his pals at nursery, David will not be going to primary school. You see, he is dying of an incurable . . .'
- **A cryptic comment** – An opener that appears to have no relevance to the story may get readers reading on to discover the connection.

Make sure your opener is relevant to your reader. Take this, which I wrote for a daily newspaper:

> We hear from time to time about doctors being struck off. It is the ultimate punishment for a doctor found guilty of gross misconduct – such as having sex with a patient, killing or harming someone in their care by administering the wrong drug, or committing some other major error or misdemeanour. But we never hear about the patients who are struck off. Unlike doctors, patients don't need to commit an offence for it to happen to them. And unlike the doctors, they don't get a hearing and they can't appeal. They don't even have the right to find out why they were struck off.

The article focuses on patients because more patients than doctors read national newspapers. Here's another article I wrote on the same subject, this time for a specialist publication aimed at general practitioners (family doctors):

> Imagine this. It's Monday morning at your surgery. Your receptionist comes in with your coffee and post. Just an ordinary day. A GMC frank

catches your eye and you open the envelope. The letter tells you that you have been struck off their register. Surely there must be some mistake? You have done nothing wrong. There's been no hearing. To your knowledge, there have been no complaints about you. You reach for the phone. The GMC will not reveal why you have been struck off, they do not want to hear what you have to say, you have no right to an appeal and you must accept the decision – which comes into effect in just seven days. How would you feel if that happened to you? Now you know how the tens of thousands of people involuntarily removed from their GPs' lists each year feel. Bewildered. Shocked. Incredulous.

In each case the article is on the same subject, but the approach taken is tailored to the audience and their experiences.

In each of these articles case histories brought the issue to life. I described real people, how they came to be struck off, and their feelings about the experience. Case histories are a valuable technique in feature writing. Use them to bring a human touch to a feature that might otherwise be too abstract or issue-based to elicit the right reader response. Consider opening your piece with one person's experience, then move on to discuss wider issues.

Types of reader

Be mindful of your readers' willingness to tackle your piece. In today's sound-bite culture, there is a growing reluctance to read anything that looks lengthy or complex. However much you abhor this trend, recognise it and cater for the needs of 21st century readers. Assume that your article will not be read from start to finish: if it is, that's a bonus. Use various tricks to cater for the three main types of reader:

- **Scanners** – Many readers begin by scanning, reading on only if something stands out and grabs their attention. Include interesting subheads to lure scanners.
- **Dippers** – These will read the bits that stand out: callouts, boxes, bulletpoints, charts and tables, etc. To cater for them, include some of your information in boxes and other forms that they find easy to digest.
- **Readers** – Yes, there are wonderful people who will actually read what you write! However, even they will start with a scan, before deciding to read on from start to finish.

The end

Some people find that stopping can be every bit as difficult as starting. Articles should have a nice, rounded ending: abrupt, sudden closures

tip

You may be asked to write on a dull subject. I have read gripping features on the dullest subjects and dreary articles on potentially mind-blowing topics. Whatever your theme, write with feeling. Ensure your enthusiasm, empathy, anger, sadness, happiness or other emotion is conveyed. Let it infect your reader.

are a sign of the inexperienced writer. Where you have developed a clear theme or hypothesis throughout your article, you should reach an end quite naturally. If you are struggling, here are some ideas for bringing your article to a conclusion:

- **Look to the future** – A short muse about future trends of your subject can round off an article.
- **Refer back** – A conclusion that refers back to your opening paragraph can complete the circle.
- **Ask a question** – A rhetorical question to leave the reader pondering.

Start powerfully, round off neatly, and fill the middle with interesting prose. That's the secret of a good article.

Newsletters

Many organisations produce staff and customer/supporter newsletters. Too many are little more than organisational propaganda, and are discarded unread by a sceptical audience. This chapter shows how to put together a really readable newsletter. It suggests story ideas and shows how to mix long and short pieces.

This chapter covers internal publications (for staff) and external ones (for supporters/donors/members/customers). Although a staff newsletter is a different beast to one for customers, the same principles apply.

Staff newsletters

Regard staff newsletters as marketing tools to 'sell' your organisation to staff. You want their loyalty and understanding, their interest and attention. But be careful not to produce something that is seen as nothing more than organisation propaganda. A one-way vehicle for the bosses to spout the organisation's line at a disbelieving and cynical staff will do you no favours. An upbeat newsletter full of success stories will not wash with staff who are demotivated or threatened with redundancy. Staff newsletters have to be brave. They must not shirk from addressing difficult or delicate issues and from breaking bad news honestly. Nor must they be afraid to present differing viewpoints on the same issue, so that important topics are properly debated. Only then will they win the respect of staff and attract a strong following.

⊠ *ZIPCO WELL PLACED FOR FUTURE GROWTH*

A planned restructuring at Zipco will leave the company well placed to tap into new markets and to go from strength to strength. That is the view of chairman Bob Zip, who today unveiled exciting plans for the company's future.

'We are in a highly competitive market,' said Mr Zip, 'but this reorganisation will ensure that we are fit for the task ahead. Part of the restructuring will involve downsizing of around 50 per cent, making us leaner and fitter.'

> **tip**
> Effective newsletters contain a mix of snippets, short news articles and lengthier features that can delve into an issue. The mix may feature both light-hearted and serious pieces.

This is an example of the sort of corporate propaganda you should avoid. What at first appears to be good news for staff is actually dreadful. Half the workforce is to be sacked! It is hopeless trying to wrap this up in overhyped PR-speak: people are not stupid. False corporate optimism of this sort breeds anger and resentment among staff. Be open and candid when it comes to bad news. Your message might not be palatable, but it will provoke less anger if you are honest.

Content

What goes in depends on the organisation. What's right for a multi-national's newsletter will probably not be right for a tiny charity. Consider the following:

- **News** – Any developments and how they will affect the organisation's performance, future and staff.
- **Staff news** – Promotions, leavers and joiners.
- **Letters** – A letters page/column transforms a newsletter into a two-way vehicle.
- **Articles** – An opportunity to provide a more in-depth look at certain key issues.
- **Rules/requirements** – Anything staff should know about, such as the introduction of a no-smoking policy or other procedures that will affect them.
- **Information** – About holiday opening hours, staff discounts or the pension scheme.
- **Open space** – A chance for staff to sound off about something.

> **tip**
> Avoid a chairperson's or chief executive's message. Also steer clear of departmental profiles – unless they are genuinely interesting, written in a lively style and likely to be read with interest by staff in other areas. Badly drawn and boring cartoon strips and over-simple crosswords and puzzles should also be given a miss.

Customer/supporter newsletters

tip

Most contributions to your newsletter will benefit from editing or even complete rewriting. Don't be feeble when it comes to the red pen. Ensure that anything making it into print is worthy of it. Don't inflict substandard copy on readers simply because you fear that you will upset a contributor's feelings if you edit their work.

Many customer newsletters are of the 'Aren't we Great' variety. They tell the customer how fantastic the organisation is, how wonderful its equipment/procedures/services are, how great the staff are, how superb the customer service is and so on. Readers couldn't care less! No one is going to read company hype. Readers are not stupid and will not swallow wholesale everything you publish. They have no interest in you; only in what you can do for them.

Customer/supporter newsletters should do at least one of the following:

- inform in a relevant and interesting way;
- promote your products/services – but in a subtle and not too boastful way;
- sell (or raise money, if you are a charity) – softly;
- establish/maintain a relationship.

Customer newsletters have to be worth reading. If they're not, they won't be read. What a waste of time and money that would be! Newsletters written from a company perspective are ignored. Only those taking the customer's viewpoint stand a chance. So don't say how great your products are, show how they can help or have helped your customers.

⊠ HAYES SECURITY PRODUCTS

[article accompanied by photo of Hayes' chief executive]

Hayes is <u>the</u> name in home security, providing burglar alarms, window locks, door chains, spy-holes, entry phones, even CCTV. Our pedigree stretches back over a century, yet we work with leading edge technology. Hayes is an industry leader in security products, supplying over half the UK's window locks. We are the industry's most admired supplier . . .

This may be true, but so what? It's not gonna hook readers. They want something that will interest them, that will connect with their own experience, that will mean something to them. The following box is more interesting and relevant to readers.

☑ **As burglary rates soar, we show
you how to keep burglars at bay**

[article accompanied by photo of woman in ransacked house, looking distressed]

SAFE AS HOUSES?

It's everyone's worst nightmare. You get back from holiday to find your home's been trashed. Papers everywhere. Furniture upturned. Even the kids' playroom ransacked. This is the scene Jenny Smith from Windsor found when she returned from a fortnight in the Algarve. Her home had been burgled and all her jewellery stolen. The cameo brooch from her grandmother, her diamond eternity ring, all her gold, her christening bracelet, the lot. Gone.

'For months I dreaded leaving the house, even for a few minutes,' says Jenny. 'I became paranoid. It was affecting my health. Eventually I got round to doing something about it. The local Crime Prevention Officer came round and suggested that I improve my home security – burglar alarm, window locks, that kind of thing. So I did. I had a Hayes Home Protector fitted and it's the best thing I ever did. Now I sleep at night. I leave the house and don't worry about what I'll find when I get back. It may sound over the top, but it has changed my life for the better, it really has,' says Jenny.

If you want to know how you can improve your home's security cheaply and quickly, see the article on page 4 . . .

This sort of approach clicks with readers. They can identify with the woman featured, feel sympathy with her and put themselves in her shoes. It gets them thinking. Maybe they should improve their home security. Perhaps they will read that helpful article on page 4. Then they might use the money-off vouchers mailed with the newsletter to buy some of your products. You've made a sale by being interesting and informative. You would not have done it by being trumpet-blowing or too 'corporate'.

Content

Again this depends. What will appeal for a business-to-business readership will be different from a consumer or supporter newsletter. Consider the following:

■ Different/unusual ways of using the product: recipes using your baked beans; things you can make using your glue; interior design paint effects which can be achieved using your products.

tip

Use a writing
style that shows
your newsletter's
personality.
It might be
friendly/chatty;
helpful;
informative or
authoritative.
Devise a style
and stick to it.
Ensure the
design reinforces
the style. An
informal, chatty
newsletter should
look different to
a more serious,
authoritative one.

- Helpful hints.
- 'How to' features – how to get a bigger pension; how to improve your health; how to get help with your fuel bills.
- Case histories/human interest.
- Seasonal stories – Christmas, Easter, summer hols.
- Your questions answered.
- Feedback – reader feedback and your response to it.
- Calendar/diary/forthcoming events – New season's clothes arrive; fundraising events; fashion show; summer sale; open day.

Cover page

Your cover page should have a lead article accompanied, if possible, by a strong photograph. Use a bold headline to attract attention and give your newsletter 'pick-me-up' appeal. For tips on how the lead story, headline and photo work together, pick up any newspaper. See how they do it. Consider a contents box too. Even if your newsletter is just four pages long, it can still include one. This serves to draw the reader in and gets them to open up the newsletter. Work hard on getting your front page right because if it looks unattractive or uninviting, your reader is unlikely to look beyond it.

tip

You want readers to get to know your publication and look forward to receiving it. If each newsletter looks completely different from the last, you may find yourself starting from scratch in building up a following. Aim for familiarity, so that readers recognise your newsletter, but keep it fresh too. Try to have regular features so that readers learn their way about the newsletter. Use a familiar design and layout too.

Annual reports

Annual reports from both the commercial and voluntary sectors have improved dramatically over the last two decades, but there are still plenty which leave a great deal of room for improvement. This chapter will show how to produce exciting, different, mould-breaking, lively and effective annual reports that actually get read.

Do you regard the production of the annual report as a chore? You are not alone! It will always be boring to produce if all you ever come up with is a dreary account of your organisation's activities, followed by pages of unintelligible figures.

Annual reports have two main types of reader:

1. **Those with a professional interest** – There are some poor souls who have to read annual reports, however dry and dull. This group includes bankers, City analysts and people from grant-making bodies and trusts.
2. **Those with a passing interest** – This might include shareholders, staff, supporters and others receiving a report. They have some interest in the organisation and will flick through a report, but you'll need to persuade them to give it more than a glance.

Satisfy the professional reader and their need for the nitty gritty of the year's activities, but don't overlook the interests of other potential readers. If you can finance it, why not produce two reports:

■ A full annual report and accounts (for the professionals).
■ An abridged report (for others), which includes an advert for the full version for those who would like it.

> **tip**
> You may not be able to afford two printed versions, but how about offering a full and an abridged version online? By producing two reports you can tailor the copy for the reader. Each gets what they want, in a form that they can digest. If the printed production of two reports is not feasible, split the report in two. Keep it interesting and lively at the front, with all the statutory stuff at the back. That way everyone's happy.

Legal requirements

You must fulfil certain legal requirements, which vary depending on whether you are:

- a public listed company;
- an unlisted company;
- a small business (according to your turnover, number of staff and balance sheet);
- a charity (there are varying requirements for different types of charity, depending on their status and on whether they are also limited companies. Additionally there are differences for Scottish charities.)

It is impossible to cover all of the various requirements here, which are governed by legislation (such as the Companies Act 1985, Statements of Standard Accounting Practice, Statement of Recommended Practice Accounting by Charities etc.). While many of the requirements relate to the figures in annual accounts, some concern the narrative. Depending on the status of your company or organisation, you might be required to include:

- a Chairperson's statement;
- directors' reports;
- disclosure of certain information about future activities, research and development, and other plans;
- activities and results.

Most reports follow a formula, starting with a chairperson's report, followed by a series of statements by the chief executive, the finance director and other directors. Inevitably this approach is dull, disjointed and potentially repetitive. A way around this is to develop a theme for the report. Explain the theme to each director. Ask them to tell you about progress related to the themes. Gather the raw data and turn it into flowing copy that hangs together. Ensure each director's report links with the next one, while avoiding boring repetition.

> **tip**
>
> Talk to your company secretary (if you have one) or to your auditors to establish the requirements for your organisation. While not all requirements will apply to your organisation, you might regard it as good practice to follow them in any case. There's also advice online at such websites as www.charity-commission.gov.uk and www.companieshouse.gov.uk.

> **tip**
>
> Just because most reports are rather staid productions, there's no need for yours to be. Don't be a slave to convention: let your creativity dictate how the report should be. Don't be afraid to try a new approach, such as producing a report that is a glossy magazine, a comic (great for a kids' charity), a poster, even a carrier bag! Dare to be different. Break the mould and produce something that makes people sit up and take notice.

With a shelf-life of a whole year, it's worth spending effort getting your annual report right. Take your time and start at least six months before publication date if you want a comfortable schedule. Devise potential ideas and themes. Try them out on others. Start planning the content at an early stage. Soon the report will take shape without too much effort.

One of the greatest challenges is to present the accounts section in a way that is meaningful to the average reader. It might be crystal clear to the accountants and auditors, but most people give up when faced with complex balance sheets. If you want your finances understood, present them so they make sense. Enhance the balance sheet with user-friendly charts and graphics, attractively designed, to show at a glance what the figures mean. Or add a plain English commentary to explain the finances.

Another perceived challenge is that of cramming a year's work into a few pages. Don't try to cram it all in. Select key highlights and use them to give a flavour. That's better than packing pages with every last detail, regardless of whether or not it will be read. Include bulletpointed lists too, where appropriate, rather than narrative.

Exclude unnecessary lists, then add a bit of life to any that remain. Don't just state the names of directors – add a little interest by telling the reader something about the people behind the names.

☒ *John Smith*
  Mary Taylor
  Rajiv Ram

☑ **John Smith**
  As well as serving on our Board, John is also a director of Jeeve's Champagne. You will see that this year we have introduced champagne truffles to our range of luxury chocolates, thanks to John's links with Jeeve's.

  Mary Taylor
  Food writer Mary Taylor has been on our Board for six years . . .

Although the annual report and accounts is a legal requirement for many, use it as a marketing tool to inform, educate, persuade, reassure, motivate, impress. Think about how you can turn raw information about your organisation's performance into a powerful and persuasive document. Achieve this by:

■ lively and readable copy;
■ lots of bite-size chunks of copy in preference to dense text;
■ great photos and good design;
■ good use of captions;
■ being outward-looking, not inward-looking;
■ focusing on what your products/services do for people, not how they came about;
■ adding human interest.

tip

Get hold of other reports. Study the content, style, design and presentation of financial information. What do you like? What ideas can you adapt? Make a note of what to avoid.

tip

Ensure that your report encapsulates what you stand for as an organisation. Copy and design must work together to convey your organisation's philosophy, personality and principles. Give a snapshot of the year, but show how that relates to past years and to future years. Leave the reader with a real feel for what you are about, and an interest in finding out more next year.

Catalogues

All copywriting assignments require planning, but none more so than the catalogue. This chapter shows you how to plan a catalogue and how to write catalogue entries that sell products.

The catalogue is the supreme selling tool. It has to do the job of the sales assistant, singing the virtues of a product and persuading people to part with their money. As the product is not in front of the potential customer, the catalogue has to make up for this deficiency. Some challenge, and all using just a few words and pictures!

There are four types of catalogue:

1. **Descriptive** – This shows the goods and offers a straightforward description of the product, limiting itself largely to the essentials (size, colour, materials). A typical entry might read:

   Polo shirt
   100% cotton. Navy, white and black. Sizes S, M, L, XL. Machine washable.
   £16.99

2. **Descriptive plus** – Catalogue entries tend to be brief. These offer a bit more than the basic minimum description. Generally a little persuasive sales patter is thrown in to enhance the description:

   Polo shirt
   A classic that no man's wardrobe should be without. Our polo shirt features authentic rib collar and cuffs (often omitted on cheaper impostors) and quality top-stitching to create a more robust garment. 100% cotton. Navy, white and black. Sizes S, M, L, XL. Machine washable. £16.99

3. **Magalogue** – This is a cross between a catalogue and a magazine. Containing relevant articles as well as catalogue entries, it provides the shopper with more of a read. It might include features on the designers whose goods are featured in the catalogue, or perhaps on the countries where the items come from. Some magalogues even feature guest writers. Its aim is to interact more with the reader and to make them feel more involved with the products.
4. **Specialogue** – This is a very specialist catalogue catering for a niche market and offering specialist products.

TRUE STORY

Magalogues offer more scope for the copywriter. Even quite ordinary products can provide an opportunity for interesting, relevant and readable articles. A menswear catalogue featured the button-down shirt – using 1950s and '60s nostalgic images such as photos of pop group The Who and other icons of that era, and some great copy to accompany them. A tile manufacturer carried articles by experts on historic Moorish, Islamic and Victorian tiles. Enliven a catalogue in this way and add credibility too: if experts are willing to write in your catalogue on rare Islamic tiles, doesn't that say something about the standing of your products?

Devise a logical order for your catalogue. A clothing catalogue could be organised under menswear, women's wear and children's clothing, or according to garment type (trousers, shoes, coats and so on). Decide what to include, in addition to product descriptions. Will there be any articles? Do you need to include instructions on how to order, how to measure, how to get refunds? An index? An order form? Addresses and phone numbers? Draw up a list so that you don't forget anything.

Providing reassurance

Consider how to convey confidence in your company or charity, especially if you are not already a household name. Customers contemplating ordering from an unknown organisation will look for evidence that you are *bona fide*:

- Include soothing words to reassure.
- Highlight any guarantees and money-back offers.
- Add anything else that will calm customers.
- Include information about the company or charity, such as how long you have been trading or (in the case of charity catalogues) what work you undertake and how the profits will be spent.

Leaflets

Find out about different leaflet types and what to include in each. Discover how to devise an irresistible, page-turning front cover that will ensure your leaflet is picked up and read.

By its nature, a leaflet is short: generally no more than a couple of sides of A4, but often just half that! Allowing for photos, illustrations and 'white space' you may find yourself left with room for just 400–500 words – less still on an A5 leaflet. (To give you an indication of how long that is, this paragraph is nearly 100 words.) It's tough trying to fit it all into so few words. Every word counts. Every illustration must add information. You will need to focus on two or three key points. Everything else must be omitted.

Most leaflets fall into one of these categories:

■ general purpose leaflets;
■ information leaflets;
■ sales leaflets;
■ booking leaflets.

General purpose leaflets

These explain very broadly what you do as an organisation, what you stand for or what you believe in. It's difficult trying to cover everything without getting too wordy. It can be best simply to present a flavour of what you do rather than go into the detail, so that readers are left feeling that they like you. They don't need to know everything about you in order to feel good about you. Refer readers to your brochures, catalogues or website if they want further information.

Information leaflets

Leaflets created to inform ('All your insurance questions answered' or 'How your donation will help') are easiest to write. The 'questions and answers' format works well here. You pose the questions that the reader will want addressed, then go on to answer them.

Sales leaflets

For sales leaflets to sell, they must contain a call to action or a mechanism to enable easy response. This might be in the form of an order form or a coupon – or simply the inclusion of your address (or website), opening hours and directions, if appropriate.

Booking leaflets

These are leaflets designed to publicise and encourage bookings for a conference, training course, fundraising event or similar. Aim to make such leaflets as easy to reply to as possible, perhaps by using a tear-off slip. Make sure that you:

■ include the return address on the tear-off slip;
■ don't put any essential information on the back of the slip;
■ include a cut-off date for applications/bookings.

The front cover

People do judge books (and leaflets!) by their covers. Make sure yours is arresting if you want to increase the chances of the leaflet being read. Design influences the impact of a leaflet, but so does copy. Well chosen words can help attract that all-important attention. The wrong choice of words could switch off your intended readership and lose you valuable custom or support.

☒ *Historic homes in England*

This straight factual approach *might* attract the attention of people interested in historic homes. It will not hold any appeal for those who don't see themselves as historic homes type of people. The approach below should do the trick:

☑ *Want ideas for:*

• *Fun days out in England?*
• *Beautiful gardens to visit?*

- *The most picturesque picnic spots in England?*
- *Gorgeous houses full of history and treasures which you can poke around in?*

Such an approach enables you to catch the interest of people who may not label themselves as interested in historic homes, but who like a good day out. It offers you a chance to persuade them, by talking in their language and recognising their needs.

The front cover must achieve a dual purpose. First it must attract attention, so that the leaflet is noticed and picked up. Next it must foster interest, so that the leaflet is opened and read. If you are sharing the secrets of eternal youth, or 20 ways to get rich quick, chances are that you will have little trouble in attracting the necessary attention and fostering interest! The subject matter is powerful enough to do the work for you. But what if you are selling life insurance, pension plans, or other less 'sexy' subjects?

[x] *Life Insurance*

[x] *Pension Plans*

These headlines are unlikely to produce the desired effect, unless the reader is actively seeking those products. Find a different way of capturing the interest of your reader – by being cryptic and using ellipses. Take the life insurance leaflet:

[✓] *[front cover]*
  In the time it takes you to read this . . .

  [inside the leaflet]
  . . . over 100 people in Britain will have died. Fewer than half of them will have had life insurance.

Now for the pension plan leaflet:

[✓] *[front cover]*
  Travelling abroad to exotic locations. Shopping at lovely boutiques. Eating out in good restaurants.

  [inside the leaflet]
  Is this how you will spend your retirement? Without a good pension plan, life after 60 could be very different. Poverty. A cold and damp home. Struggling to pay the bills. Which scenario would you prefer?

Both leaflets lure the reader. The front cover is interesting, unlike a direct appeal to take out a pension or insurance. Each enables the reader to consider the drawbacks of life without these products.

tip

When producing a leaflet, it helps to know its format before you begin to write. You can then plan your blocks of text to fit the space. The majority of leaflets are:

- A4 landscape folded in half (four pages of A5);
- A4 landscape folded twice (six pages each of which is a third of A4);
- A5.

Leaflets can be printed on larger or smaller sheets or folded in all sorts of fancy ways. Select the format that is best for the amount of copy you have, and that fits the budget. Then plan your copy around it.

Everything else!

This final chapter deals with a range of small writing assignments that do not merit a chapter to themselves, important as they are. Find out how to write clear instructions, how to write for foreigners, how to write coupons and response mechanisms . . . and lots more.

Coupons and response mechanisms

You may need to produce some form of coupon or response mechanism for your ads, mailshots, leaflets and so forth. Bear the following in mind when drawing up your coupon response:

1. Ensure the wording elicits all the information you need or want from your respondent.
2. Repeat the offer – 'Yes, please rush me a copy of your free brochure . . .'.
3. If using coupons in different publications, code them in the bottom corner so you can tell which publication triggered which response. This enables you to assess which publication produced the best response.
4. Leave enough space. Make sure the coupon is big enough for respondents to complete with ease. If they have to squash their details in they may give up, or you may have trouble reading their writing.

tip

Put your return address on the coupon rather than in the body of the ad/leaflet. (Readers who lose the ad or brochure will still know where to send the coupon.)

Instructions

Have you ever struggled to build self-assembly furniture? The problem often lies in the way the instructions are written. They don't seem to be clear and logical, they may be ambiguous and they are generally very difficult to follow. Yet writing instructions is not difficult. You may have to write instructions from time to time. Take on board the following points when writing yours.

1. Put yourself into the reader's shoes. What knowledge or background information will they have already? What can you take for granted and what will you need to explain?
2. Identify any words and expressions that you must explain in order to enable someone to follow your instructions. You can use footnotes or a glossary to explain these, or you can include an explanation in the main text.
3. Where appropriate, begin with an instruction advising the reader to read through the full instructions before getting started.
4. Follow a logical order. Numbered steps can work well. This way the reader knows that they must complete Step 1 before moving on to Step 2.
5. Where instructions are long and complex, it may help to break them up into manageable sections.
6. Consider including a checklist at the beginning of your instructions, perhaps listing everything the reader will need in order to complete the form (or build the bookcase!) For example:

   Before completing this form you will need:

   - *Your child's birth certificate*
   - *A letter from the head teacher at your child's current school*
   - *The full address of the new school you wish your child to attend.*

7. Include a checklist at the end if it will help the reader check that everything has been completed and that they have not overlooked or forgotten anything important. For example:

   Remember to enclose:

   - *Your rent book*
   - *A cheque made payable to Anytown Housing Association*
   - *A stamped envelope with your own name and address on it.*

8. Include a list of the contents if appropriate.
9. Consider saying how long it will take to complete, if appropriate.
10. Include a trouble-shooting guide.
11. Consider using a few examples to help explain to the reader exactly what you mean.
12. Ask yourself whether diagrams, photographs or other illustrations would be better than words. Or use visuals in conjunction with words. A clear and carefully labelled diagram identifying the various parts referred to in the instructions can be a great

help. Be sure to use the same labels in the text as in the diagram – don't refer to 'Board A' in the text, when it is labelled 'Piece A' in the diagram.

13. Think about whether a flow chart would be best. This is generally good when there are several stages where the instructions path will divide, depending on whether the reader answers 'yes' or 'no'.

14. Keep it simple, but never over-simplify and leave the reader lacking vital information. It can be a difficult balance to achieve. Include everything that is necessary, but try to identify anything that it unnecessary and leave that out.

Aim for clarity and brevity. If you can shorten sentences by cutting out unnecessary words, do so.

☒ *Take the piece labelled 'a' on the enclosed diagram and attach it (using the screwdriver provided) to piece B*

☑ *Screw piece B to piece A.*

Be as precise as necessary, to prevent doubt in the reader's mind.

☒ *Place in a hot oven.*

☑ *Place in an oven preheated to 220 degrees centigrade (Gas Mark 7).*

When you have finished writing your instructions, set them aside for a day or two before re-reading. Make any improvements that are necessary, then ask a colleague to read through them with a critical eye, or consider asking someone to follow your instructions to see if they work. Amend instructions in the light of any exposed ambiguity or lack of clarity.

---

tip

Sometimes instructions benefit from a FAQ (frequently asked questions) section. Anticipate questions you believe readers may wish to ask and answer them at the end of the instructions. This Q&A format can be very effective in addressing readers' questions and saving them the trouble of having to get in touch with you.

Packaging

Product packaging (box, carton, labels) represents a great marketing opportunity for the copywriter. Too often packaging is seen as a design challenge: regard it as shared terrain, with you and the designer or packaging specialist working together. Attractive packaging can sell a product – I am a sucker for anything that comes in a glittery box – but the words on that packaging are important too. There may be legislative requirements you will need to comply with. Check them out. You may need to list:

- ingredients;
- country of manufacture;
- weight;
- nutritional information;
- materials;
- 'CE' kitemark and other accreditations;
- warnings (Keep away from naked flames/Keep out of reach of children);
- storage information/advice;
- contents;
- address;
- guarantee.

Aside from any statutory requirements, there's the opportunity for some creativity. The challenge is to write appealing prose that will fit neatly into the small space available on a label or box. There's little point is simply stating what's inside; do a bit of sales patter.

☒ *Seven bars of glycerine soap*

☑ *Seven bars of pure glycerine soap in all the colours of the rainbow.*

> *Hand-made by monks in the Alyserian hills, using traditional techniques that have not changed since the time of Jesus.*

> *Pure, clean and gently fragranced.*

It's the same soap, but now it sounds a more interesting proposition. There's a bit of history attached to it, and more product information too. Obviously it is easier to write colourful copy for interesting products. What if you are writing packaging for motor oil, nuts and bolts, or spanners? The same rule applies: make the product sound interesting.

☒ *This pack contains two domestic grade spanners suitable for DIY use.*

☑ **Two spanners ideal for DIY.**
> *Booker's Spanners are made of top grade steel (the same steel we use for our 'Professional' range), so they won't rust.*

> *Guaranteed to provide years of trouble-free use.*

You can see that packaging is not simply a device to list contents; it's an opportunity to persuade and to sell.

Captions

Write captions with as much thought as you give the body copy. Too often, captions (to illustrations and photographs) are added as an afterthought. Regard them as an integral part of the copy. They are far more likely to be read than the body copy, so their role is vital. A caption that merely repeats what the illustration shows is a wasted opportunity. The role of the caption is to add information, not repeat it. Suppose you were carrying a photograph of the footballer Thierry Henry in your marketing material:

☒ *Thierry Henry*

Far better to make the most of the opportunity with something like:

☑ *Top footballer Thierry Henry insists on the best. That's why he wears Hi-Star trainers on and off the pitch.*

Do not limit your caption to just two or three words. Extended captions can be used to good effect, running to three or even four sentences.

Notices

Most notices make two mistakes:

■ they contain too much text;
■ they lack an attention-grabbing headline.

☒ *We would like our customers to note that batches of Bobby's Babyfood bought at this store during April may contain small pieces of rubber, due to equipment failure at the manufacturers. If you have bought any Bobby's Babyfood at this store in April, please return it to us for a full refund. Under no circumstances should you use the product. We apologise for any alarm or inconvenience. If you have any questions or concerns, please ask any member of staff if you can speak to the store manager.*

☑ *URGENT PRODUCT RECALL*
Bobby's Babyfood

If you bought Bobby's Babyfood at this store during April, please return it to us immediately. It may contain pieces of rubber. You will be given a full refund. We apologise for any alarm or inconvenience this recall may cause. Please ask to see the store manager if you have any questions or concerns.

The second version attracts attention with its main headline and narrows the audience with the secondary headline. It is less wordy and thus clearer.

Posters

Many of the rules for notices apply to posters too. Keep it brief, bold and simple. Use a strong and attention-grabbing headline. Include all the pertinent information, or details of how to find out more.

> ☒ *ANYTHORPE VILLAGE CARNIVAL*
>
> *Anythorpe Village is delighted to announce that its traditional annual carnival will take place again this year. As usual there will be plenty for the whole family, with fairground rides, pony rides, stalls, food and lots more besides. So be there for the event of the year!*
>
> *Village Green, Anythorpe. Saturday May 24 from 2pm to 5pm.*

> ☑ *ANYTHORPE VILLAGE CARNIVAL*
>
> | *Family fun* | *Fairground rides* | *Stalls* |
> |---|---|---|
> | *Pony rides* | *Food* | *Lots more too!* |
>
> *Village Green, Anythorpe. Saturday May 24 from 2pm to 5pm.*

It is easier to take in a few words than to digest full sentences, particularly when read at a distance or on the move, as most posters will be.

Speech-writing

Speeches are written to be read aloud, making them a very different proposition from a press advert or a brochure. You should try to capture the informality and vitality of the spoken word in every copy-writing assignment, but nowhere is this more true than when writing a speech. Tortured speeches are as painful for the audience as for the speaker. Stilted or awkward phrases delivered with a monotonous voice are guaranteed to produce yawns, if not snores!

DOS AND DON'TS FOR SPEECH WRITERS

DO

☑ As your writing will be read out loud, do use the ordinary language that you would when speaking.

☑ Adopt a style that will suit the audience and the event. A humorous speech at a rather stuffy event might be out of place (or could be a refreshing change!)

☑ Use humour with care. There is nothing worse than jokes that no one laughs at, allusions no one understands, and wit that causes embarrassment.

☑ Make your points clearly. When people don't understand something they have read, they can reread it to clarify the point. With a speech, listeners have to get your points the first time. They can't 're-listen'.

DON'T

☒ Try to make too many points – it will confuse the audience. Research shows that people remember very little from speeches.

☒ If writing for someone else, don't use words or phrases that they would not use. Write in a style appropriate for the speaker.

You need to grab attention within the first 30 seconds (the first challenge) and then hold attention for the rest of the speech (the second, and possible greater challenge). Consider opening with a thought-provoking question that will engage the audience, include a relevant anecdote or a controversial statement that will get ears pricked up and listening.

Close a speech with a summary of the main points and possibly some further food for thought that will leave them with a positive memory of the speaker.

Writing for foreigners

Most foreigners are not fluent in English. When writing for them (information leaflets for hotels, tourist information material, publicity for an international exhibition) bear the following points in mind:

tip
Sentences that are easy to read in your head may not flow when you read them aloud. Reread your speech aloud before editing, so you can spot what needs to be rephrased.

- If someone's first language is not English, they are unlikely to understand colloquialisms, slang and abbreviations.
- They will find shorter words and sentences easier to cope with.
- They may use a dictionary to aid translation. Try to select words that do not have too many possible meanings.
- Clichés may be taken literally!

TRUE STORY

In the 1850s Pedro Carolino and Jose da Fonseca decided to write an English phrasebook, 'Guide to the Conversation in Portuguese and English'. Problem was, they didn't speak English and didn't have a Portuguese-English dictionary! They did have a Portuguese-French dictionary, and a French-English dictionary. Using these, they translated the Portuguese expressions into French, then the French into English. Inevitably quite a lot got lost in translation! The results are hilarious. Examples include: 'A bad arrangement is better than a process' and 'Take out the live coals with the hand of the cat'. The book, published under the title *English as She is Spoke* is still a bestseller today.

APPENDIX

Improvement in writing ability

In the first chapter you were asked to assess your writing ability by completing a quick questionnaire. Now let's see if you are any happier with your copywriting skills than you were when you started this book. If you have read the book thoroughly, taken on board the tips and worked through the exercises, you should find that you are much more confident and capable.

Current writing ability: self-assessment test

Complete the questionnaire again. Then compare the results with the questionnaire you filled in at the front of the book.

1. I would rate my writing ability as:

a) Poor.
b) Slightly below average.
c) Average.
d) Slightly above average.
e) Good.
f) Excellent.

2. I find getting started:

a) Impossible.
b) Very difficult.
c) Fairly hard.
d) Not hard, but not easy.
e) Fairly easy.
f) Very easy.

3. When I am asked to write some marketing or fundraising material I feel:

a) A sense of dread and panic.

b) Genuinely worried that I will make a mess of it.

c) That it will be a struggle and will take time, but I will be able to come up with something, albeit second-rate.

d) That I will do an OK job, but not a great one.

e) That I will be able to produce a good piece of work in a reasonable timeframe.

f) That it will be a doddle and the output will be great.

4. I think that the publicity material I write is:

a) Dreadful.

b) Poor.

c) Average.

d) Good but could be improved.

e) Above average.

f) Excellent.

5. When it comes to words and language:

a) I have no interest whatsoever in words and how they work.

b) I'm not that interested in words, but very occasionally I will look at a piece of publicity and wonder how the creators came up with the concept.

c) I have an average interest in words – no more and no less than an average person.

d) From time to time I look at/analyse/think about other people's creative work.

e) I enjoy reading and thinking about professional copy and find myself doing it frequently.

f) I am very interested in words and I find language fascinating.

6. When it comes to writing marketing and fundraising material (donor letters, press ads, brochures, annual reports):

a) I find it difficult to write anything and always feel dissatisfied with the end result.

b) I have trouble getting started and rarely like the finished material.

c) I can write some types of marketing material to a reasonable standard, but find others considerably more difficult.

d) I can write most types of material competently, but feel there's room for improvement.

e) I am confident that I can tackle most assignments without too much difficulty and can produce good work.

f) I can turn my hand to anything with ease, always producing very good work.

7. How long does it take you to write, say, a one page fundraising letter, or some other short piece of marketing material, to a good standard?

a) It takes me far too long. I have trouble getting started; I pore over it and never feel that it is any good.

b) It takes me a lot longer than it should, but I get there in the end.

c) I take a bit longer than I would like and feel there is room for improvement.

d) My speed is OK.

e) I can produce good work within an acceptable timescale.

f) I can turn out quality work quickly and easily.

Scores

Now add up your score. Award yourself:

One point for every a) you ticked
Two for every b)
Three for a c)
Four for a d)
Five for an e)
Six for an f)

Assessment

Refer back to page 8. Read the paragraph that refers to your score.

You should see an improved score. Having seen how much you have improved, you will gain in confidence and take on more demanding copywriting assignments. The more you do, and the more you are stretched, the better you will become. The better you become, the more you will enjoy writing and the more you will want to take on. By this stage you will have developed your own style and will write quite naturally and a lot less painfully. Keep it up and that day will be just round the corner. Good luck!

Index

abbreviations 46, 124, 164
action 13, 80, 108, 109, 117, 118,
    127, 155 *see also* response
    adrenaline 28
active voice 36
adjectives 86
advertising 3–5 *passim*, 7, 32, 52,
    55, 59–62 *passim*, 64, 70,
    72–8 *passim*, 80, 82, 95,
    98–100, 116–27, 163, 167
    AIDA formula 116–18
    British Code of 125–6
    Broadcasting Codes 125
    bus 34, 126
    classifieds 124–5
    'period' style 88–9
    print 117–26
    radio 126–7
    'reading' 118–19
    Standards Authority 72–4
        passim, 125
afternoons, avoidance of 29
age 57
alcohol 28
alliteration 58, 89
ambiguity 26, 60, 69–70, 159, 160
annual reports 7, 10, 88, 89,
    148–51, 167
    abridged version 149
    accounts section 151
    readership 149
antonyms 62–3
anxiety 3, 5
apostrophes 45–7
    Protection Society 46
articles 59, 83, 140–3, 145, 153
assessment, self- 3, 5–8, 166–8
assonance 60
attention 73, 117, 155, 156, 163,
    164
audience 9–12, 17, 116, 140–2,
    163, 164
    identifying 9–12

Balzac, Honoré de 85
benefits 11, 12, 14, 15, 18, 22, 70
body copy 115, 119, 122–3, 162
    dos and don'ts 123
boxes 11, 38–40, 142
brainstorming 29
break, taking a 28, 29
breaks, word/page/line 102
brevity 26, 35, 50, 123, 130, 138,
    154, 160, 163
brief 16–19
British Airways 99
British Telecom 99
brochures 3, 7, 12, 55, 76–7,
    79–80, 109, 154, 163, 167
Brown, Dan 28
bulletpoints 11, 37–8, 113, 129,
    130, 142, 151

calligrammes 99
callouts 38, 142
capital letters, use of 45, 96, 131
captions 102, 119, 123, 151, 162
Carolino, Pedro 165
case histories 141–2, 147
catalogues 78, 81–2, 109, 152–3
    content 152–3
    descriptive 152; plus 152
    magalogue 153
    specialogue 153
chairperson's statement 150
change of assignment 28
charities 4, 74, 145, 146, 150,
    153
charts 101, 142, 151
checking 101–3
checklists 14, 18
    instruction 159
children's story 86
chunks, readable, of text 26,
    37–42, 129, 151
clarity 160
    lack of 26

clichés 26, 68–9, 82, 93, 164
    marketing 69
colleagues, consulting 29
collective nouns 85, 91
colloquialisms 164
colons 44
colours 117
commas 44
    inverted 48
Companies Act (1985) 150
competition 116, 117
conclusion 142–3
consistency 26, 101–2, 148
contact name 138
content 4, 145, 159, 161
    box 148, 159
context 140
contractions, use of 33
controversy 74
copy awareness 75–9
    bad copy 12, 16, 31, 32, 34, 36,
        37, 51, 52, 55, 59, 66–71
        passim, 73, 76–82, 111, 123,
        124, 129, 131,
        135–7 *passim*, 145, 146, 151,
        155, 160–4 *passim*
    good copy 3–4, 12, 16, 31, 32,
        34, 36, 37, 40–2 *passim*, 51,
        52, 55, 61–3 *passim,* 68,
        78–83, 96, 111, 113, 115,
        118, 120–5, 129–31, 135–7
        passim, 141–2, 147, 151,
        155–6, 160–4 *passim*
    situational copy 33–4
copying, e-mail 130
coupons 114, 155, 158
    coding 158
cover 23, 148, 154–6
creativity 4, 5, 84–93, 150, 161
credit card payment 25, 114
critical skills 75–83
crossword clues 87–8
customers 10, 11, 16, 71, 146–8
Cutts, Martin 36

deadlines 29, 30, 112, 140
death 73
demonstrating 32–3
description, powers of 92
design 4, 25, 94–103, 117, 123–4,
    138–9, 148, 151, 155

designers, working with 100
desire 118
deviance, unexpected 63
devices, graphological 95–9
diagrams 101, 159–60
dictating 28
dippers 142
direct mail 107–15 *see also*
    mailshots
directors' reports 150
disability 57
discipline 29
dishonest copy 73
donors 10, 11
dos and don'ts 35, 123, 129–31,
    134, 163–4
double spacing 138
drafting 23–5, 141

editing 22, 26–8 *passim*, 65, 102,
    146
ellipsis 61, 156
e-mails 130–1
    dos and don'ts 130–1
emotions 15–16, 142
enclosures, mailshot 109–15
ending 142–3
English 49–52
    dos and don'ts 35
    plain 35–6, 151; Campaign 36
    spoken 50, 163
envelope, mailshot 52, 107–9, 115
    pre-paid 109, 112, 114
environment 85
evocative writing 92
exercise 28
exercises, creativity-boosting 29,
    85–93
exhibitions 4
expletives 72

familiarity 50, 67, 148
fear 3, 5, 15–16, 18
    of failure 29
features 14, 15, 140–3, 147, 148,
    153
feedback 27, 147
first person, use of 31–2, 35, 112
flow chart 160
follow-up 109, 113
Fonseca, José da 165

fonts 102
footnotes 159
foreigners, writing for 164
format 11, 138–9, 157
forthcoming events 147
Freedom of Information Act 131
freephone 114
freepost 114
fundraising letters 4, 7, 168
    material 7, 146

gender 56
get out clause 111
glossary 159
good copy 3–4, 78–9, 82–3
Gowers, Sir Ernest 68
graffiti 85
grammar 4, 43–57
    mistakes 44–8
    tests 49
guarantees 112, 153, 161
guest writers 153

headings 52, 101, 102, 119
headlines 52, 59, 60, 62, 80, 82,
    95, 115, 117, 119–22, 124,
    125, 148, 156, 162, 163
    command 122
    direct 120–1
    'how to' 121
    indirect 121
    question 121–2
Heinz 97
Henry, Thierry 162
heterophones 61–2
highlighting 95, 128–9, 153
Hirst, Damien 135, 157
homonyms 61–2
homophones 61–2
hospitality, corporate 15
humour 74, 123, 131, 164
hype 70–1, 146

I and me 48
IBM 74
ideas 84–5
    box 84
    gathering 20–1, 141
    grouping into themes 21–2, 141
    placing 22–3
    sequencing 22, 141

illustrations 22, 86, 94, 100, 119,
    123, 154, 159, 162
incomplete technique 108–9
index 153
information 11, 13, 14, 22, 145,
    146, 153, 154, 158, 159, 161
    'snack' 129
    storage 161
inspiration 29
    'box' 84
instructions 153, 158–9
interest 10, 73, 117, 156
internet 128–31
    dos and don'ts 129
inversion, of word order 26, 54
irrelevance 26, 65

jargon 11, 26, 35, 138

kitemark 161
Kwikfit 117

language 7, 91, 163, 167 *see also*
    English
    aptness of 26
    bad 72
    bias in 56–7
    evocative 92
    inclusive 56–7
    Plain – Commission 36
'leading' 94
leaflets 10, 12–13, 22–3, 109,
    154–7
    booking 155
    general purpose 154
    information 155
    sales 155
legal requirements 125–6, 150–1,
    161
legalese 35
Legat, Michael 27
length
    of e-mail 130
    of paragraph 26, 129
    of sentence 26, 35, 54, 138
    of text 26, 37, 65–7, 123, 130,
        138, 140
letters 95–9
    capitalising 45, 96, 131
    emphasising 95–7
    enlarging 96

layout 96
  and numbers 99
  repeating 95
  symbols used as 99
  uncommon 97
  used as words 99
letters (correspondence) 145
  covering 109–14
  donor 7, 167
  fundraising 4, 7, 168
  information 110, 113
  lead-generating 109, 112–13
  navigational 110, 113
  sales 4, 109–12 *passim*
limericks 90
Lipmann, Maureen 99
logo 119
Lucozade 99

made-up words 91
mailing list 3, 115
mailshots 4, 52, 77–8, 81–2,
    107–15
malapropisms 63–4
managers 11
maps 101
marketing material 7
media 3, 133–4
message 14, 108
mistakes 26, 65–74, 162
  grammatical 44–9
  typo 100–3
misunderstanding 3
misused words 52–4
Moore, Jo 131
motivation 29

neutral terms 56, 130
news angle 134–5
news releases 132–9
  dating 138
  dos and don'ts 132
  five Ws 135–7
newsletters 15, 52, 78, 79, 83,
    88–9, 144–8
  contents box 148
  cover page 148
  customer/supporter 146–8;
    content 147
  staff 144–5; content 145
notes to editors 138

notices 162–3
numbers 40, 99, 102
  sequence 101

offence 56–7, 71–4, 123
officialese 35, 66–7
Ogden, Hilda 63
omissions 26, 102
onomatopoeia 97
openers 110–11, 134, 141–2
order form 25, 28, 109, 114, 155

packaging 160–1
padding 11, 35, 65–6
Panasonic 97
paragraphs 26, 129
passive voice 35–7 *passim*
Perrier 98
personality 35
photographs 3, 32, 33, 95, 100,
    117, 148, 151, 154, 159
pictures 95, 100, 119, 135, 152
planning 9–19, 65, 150–2
pomposity 71, 80
positiveness 16
possessive pronouns 46–7
posters 163
postcripts 82, 112
pressure 29
pre-views, pre-sale 15
product names 89–90, 97
promotion 4, 5, 146
proofreading 101–3
  test 102
propaganda 144–6 *passim*
Pryce, Vincent 62
publication, type of 140
pull quotes 38
punctuation 4, 44–8
puns 59–60, 95
  visual 98
purpose 12–13, 18, 113, 140

questions 164
  and answers format 155, 160
questionnaires 6–8, 49, 109,
    166–8
quotation marks 102
quotes 137

race 56–7

readership 9–12, 140–2, 149
recursion 43
redundant words 26, 65, 67
relevance 12, 26, 141
religion 74
repetition 26, 65, 67–8, 87
reply card 109, 114–15
re-reading
    aloud 164
    after interval 26–7, 160
research 9–19
response 13, 112, 114, 155
    mechanisms 158
    'speed incentive' 114
revising 19, 26–7, 141
rewards 15–16, 18, 122
rhyme 60–1, 89
Robbins, Celia Dame 89

Sainsbury's 33
samples 109, 118
scanners 128–9, 142
self-esteem 8
sentences 54–5
    inversion 26, 54
    one-worders 54–5
sex 72–3
showing 32–3
Simon, Paul 85
singulars for plurals 44
slang 164
slogans 62, 78, 82, 89
speech-writing 163–4
    dos and don'ts 163–4
spelling 4, 97, 101, 102
splitting words 97–8
spoonerisms 64, 85
staff 144–5
stapling pages together 139
starting 6, 7, 20–30, 168
    over 27
Statements of Accounting Practice
    150
stereotypes 56–7
style 26, 140, 148, 164
subheadings 41, 52, 102, 122, 129,
    142
subject 140
summary 164
symbols 99
synonyms 87

tables 142
tact 35
targeting 107, 114, 138
tautology 67
tear-off slip 114, 155
teasing 108
techniques 31–42, 58–64
    graphological 95–9
tenses 55, 80
testimonial 111, 123
testing 19, 27, 49, 115
themes 21–2, 141, 150, 151
thesaurus 87
third person, use of 31, 32, 123,
    129, 133
threats 16
Times, The 123–4
tips 10, 26, 27, 35, 40, 46, 47, 50,
    54, 56, 58, 64, 65, 74, 84, 85,
    89, 94, 97–9 passim, 101,
    102, 108, 111, 115, 122, 123,
    127, 128, 133, 137, 138, 141,
    142, 145, 146, 148–51
    passim, 155, 157, 158, 160,
    164
tone 13, 16, 130
topical references 117
trouble-shooting guide 159
true stories 28, 43, 52, 57, 60, 70,
    72–4 passim, 85, 90, 91, 97,
    111, 125, 130, 131, 153, 165
Truss, Lynn 46–7
Twain, Mark 50
typos 100–3

UBP 116
Urdang, Laurence 89
urgency 108, 131
USP 15, 18

Vauxhall 90
verbosity 66–7
very, use of 69
visuals 159
vocabulary 49, 65, 85
vouchers 109, 146

Ws, five 135–6
waffle 22, 65–6, 123
warm-ups, word 29
warnings 161

warranty 15
website 118, 128–31, 154
Wedgwood 91
Whiskas 91
Winfrey, Oprah 33
word games 29, 85
words 50–4, 167
    concrete 51
    confident 52

familiar 50, 67
made-up 91
misused 52–4
powerful 51–2
splitting 97–8
short 50
unusual 52–4
writer's block 27
    remedies 28–30